PRAISE FOR ELISA ALBERT

"This snarling girl has got it: The voice. The voice has a backbeat and a deep supply of rueful wit, and on the top layer the voice curls around to have a look at itself questioningly. As a result, the entranced reader will follow it anywhere, even to Albany."

- JONATHAN LETHEM, AUTHOR OF *BROOKLYN CRIME NOVEL*

"I'm a hater but I like Elisa Albert, an actual genius."

—SAMANTHA IRBY, AUTHOR OF *QUIETLY HOSTILE*

"The queen of No Bullshit. The barometer of how a person can be emotionally bare and honest without being treacly or a con man."

—HEIDI JULAVITS, AUTHOR OF *DIRECTIONS TO MYSELF*

"Revolutionary."

—NPR'S MORNING EDITION

"With her roving, insatiable mind, Albert reclaims the personal as intellectual, political, and essential. She is never afraid to say what others would repress or dilute. To read her is an urgent, important call to try harder to speak truth and speak it boldly."

—MERRITT TIERCE, AUTHOR OF *LOVE ME BACK*

"Crackling and bighearted... A powerhouse [that] echoes with the truth that we find harmony when we listen first to ourselves."

—*OPRAH DAILY*

"Boils with dark humor and brutal honesty."

—*PEOPLE*

"Elisa Albert doesn't screw around. In the range and the intensity of this prose is a raw honesty I find riveting, comic (always) and ultimately moving. What I take away is a kind of joyous embrace of our common sorrows, and I'm grateful as hell to have all these essays in one place."

—PETER ORNER, AUTHOR OF *AM I ALONE HERE* AND *LOVE AND SHAME AND LOVE*

Equal parts acerbic, insouciant, insightful, and moving, *The Snarling Girl* is so tonally-rich and stylistically fluid that you'll consume page after page and still want more. Albert is a writer of immense talent, wisdom, and wit, and the way she takes on her choice of subjects (contemporary feminism, motherhood, literary ambition, and the intersections of all of the above, to name just a few) is nothing short of brilliant.

—RONE SHAVERS, AUTHOR OF *SILVERFISH*

THE SNARLING GIRL

NON-FICTION

Copyright © 2024 by Elisa Albert

Cover by Joel Amat Güell

ISBN: 9781960988065

CLASH Books

Troy, NY

clashbooks.com

For Tali Bea

Don't take it personal, they said;
  but I did, I took it all quite personal—

-TONY HOAGLAND

CONTENTS

THE SNARLING GIRL

AND OTHER ESSAYS

ELISA ALBERT

THE SNARLING GIRL
NOTES ON AMBITION

A FUNNY THING happened when I published my first book, more again when I published the second, and still more yet again with the third and fourth: People began to treat me differently. The typical exchange opens with a disinterested, "What do you do?"

"I'm a writer."

Here a very subtle sneer. "That's nice. Have you published anything?"

"Yup." Offer up the abridged CV.

Suddenly they stand up a little straighter. A light goes on in their eyes.

A moment earlier they were talking to nobody, a *nothing*, but *now* they're speaking with somebody *important*, a person who *matters*.

"Wow," they say. "That's amazing." And sometimes: "I always wanted to write a book." And sometimes: "I have a great idea for a book." And sometimes: "Maybe you can help me write my book."

This dynamic awakens a ferocious dormant animal, a snarling girl with a big mouth, too smart for her own good, nothing to lose, suffering privately. She's me at fifteen, more or less. When she is ready to stop suffering privately, she'll become a writer.

Oh *really*, she snarls. *Now* I matter? Wrong, motherfucker: I mattered *before*.

She's a little trigger-happy on the misanthropic rage, this snarling girl. She is often accused of "not living up to her potential." She is neither inspired by nor impressed with prep school. The college admissions race leaves her cold. Her over-bearing mother berates her about crappy grades and lack of ambition. (Ahh, says the snarling girl, you want to see lack of ambition!? I'll show you lack of ambition!) Where she is expected to go right, she makes a habit of veering left. She is not popular, not likely to succeed. Her salvation arrives (surely you saw this coming) in the form of books, movies, music, art. She obsessively follows the trail of breadcrumbs they leave behind. Here is a neat kind of power: she can be her own cura-tor. She can find her way from one sustaining voice to another, sniffing out what's true, what's real. In her notebooks she copies out passages from novels, essays, poems, and songs. She Sharpies the especially resonant bits on her bedroom wall. This is how she learns to trust herself, no easy feat. These are the epigraphs to the as-yet unwritten book of her life, rehearsals for the senior page she is keen to assemble. Here is companion-ship, proof that the universe is much, much bigger than her radioactive family and rich bitch west L.A. and Hebrew school and Zionist summer camp. Behold: She is not crazy! She is not alone! She is not a freak! Or, rather: she *is* crazy, she *is* alone, she *is* a freak, and she'll keep glorious company with all of these other crazy, lonely freaks.

Here are her notebooks, all in a row. They live in my study now, above shelves stacked with my books, galleys, audio-books, foreign editions, literary journals, anthologies, Literary Death Match medal, piles of newspapers and magazines in which I'm celebrated as this amazing thing: a writer. A novelist. Legit. But witness, please, no coincidence, the notebooks live *above* that stuff. Spiral-bound, leather-bound, fabric-bound. Black, pink, green, floral. *This Notebook Belongs To*: **Elisa Albert**, neatly printed in the earliest, **1992**. Fake it til you make it, honey! The notebooks have seniority. Here is how she began to forge a system of belief and belonging, to say nothing of a

THE SNARLING GIRL   3

career. Am I aggrandizing her? Probably. I am just so goddamn proud of her.

Ambition. The word itself makes me want to run and hide. It's got some inexorable pejorative stench to it, why is that? I've been avoiding this essay like the plague. I'd so much rather be writing my novel, my silly secret sacred new novel, which will take a while, during which time I will not garner new followers nor see my name in the paper nor seek an advance from the publisher nor receive the hearts and likes and dings and dongs that are supposed to keep my carnivorous cancerous ego afloat. I will simply do my work. Hole up with family and friends, live in the world as best I can, and do my work.

The work: this is what I would like to talk about. The work, not the hearts and likes and dings and dongs. And maybe I can float the possibility that the work is best when it's done nowhere near the hearts and likes and dings and dongs. Maybe I can suggest that there is plenty of time for hearts and likes and dings and dongs once the work is done, and done well. Maybe I can ever so gently point out that a lot of people seem rather addicted to the hearts and likes and dings and dongs and seem to talk about and around writing a hell of a lot more than they actually do it. Maybe we can even talk about how some self-promote so extensively and shamelessly and heedlessly and artlessly that their very names become shorthand for *how not to be*.

I mean: ambition *to what*? Toward what? For what? In the service of what? Endless schmoozing and worrying and self-promotion and maniac flattery and status anxiety and name-dropping are available to all of us in any industry, any artistic medium. That thinly (or not at all) disguised desire to *win*. To best her or him or her or him, sell more, publish more, own the internet, occupy more front tables, get tagged, have the most followers, be loudest, assume some throne. Is it because we want to believe that we are in charge of our destiny, and that if "things" aren't "happening" for us, we are failing to, like, "manifest?" Or is it because we are misguided enough to think that external validation is what counts? Or is it because of some core narcissistic injury, some failure of love we carry around like a latent virus?

Perhaps it's because knocking on doors like we're running for office is a lot easier and simpler than sitting alone with our thoughts and knowledge and experience and expertise and perspective, and struggling to shape all that into exactly the right form, during which process we take the terrible chance that we might get it right and still *no one will care*. Maybe we are misguided enough to believe that what's most important *is* that people care, *regardless* of whether we get it right. Maybe getting it right doesn't even *matter* if no one cares. Maybe *not* getting it right doesn't matter if *everyone* cares. If I write an excellent book and it's not a bestseller, did I write the excellent book? If I write a middling book and it *is* a bestseller, does that make it an excellent book? If I wander around looking for it on bookstore shelves so I can photograph it and post it online, have I done good? If I publish a book and don't heavily promote it, *did I really publish a book at all!?*

Here is what we know for sure: there is no end to want. Want is a vast universe within other vast universes. There is always more, and more again. There are prizes and grants and fellowships and lists and reviews and recognitions that elude us, mysterious invitations to take up residence at some castle in Italy. One can make a life out of focusing on what one does not have, but that's no way to live. A seat at the table is plenty. (But is it a *good* seat? At which end of the table?? Alongside whom!?)

Feeling like one does not have "enough" of anything (money, status, power, fame, recognition, shoes, name it): that's where every kind of terrible shit starts. And the benchmarks of success constantly shift. Ambition is a fool's game, its rewards fool's gold. Who is happy, asks the Talmud? She who is happy with what she has.

Fine, okay, but I've been publishing for a couple decades now. When my first book came out, I was a silly wreck. I smoothed my dress and crossed my legs and waited smugly for my whole life to change. I looked obsessively at rankings, reviews. Social media wasn't yet a thing, but I made it my business to pay close attention to reception. I was hyperaware of everything said and everything not said. The positive stuff puffed me right up, and I lay awake at night in a grip of fury about the negative. You see this a lot with first timers. It's kind of cute, from afar. *Do I matter? Do I matter? Do I matter?* Rookie mistakes. What's tragic is when you see it with second, third, fourth timers. Because that hunger for validation, for hearts and likes and blings and blongs, is supposed to be shed like skin.

Ambition: *an earnest desire for some type of achievement or distinction, as power, honor, fame, or wealth, and the willingness to strive for its attainment.* Note: we are not speaking here about trying to pay our bills, have a decent place to live, buy decent food, access decent health care, get a decent education. For the purposes of this particular discussion, those fundamentals must be assumed. And there's nothing in there about spiritual betterment, social service, love, or happiness. The entire concept can therefore be seen as anti-feminist. An ideal matriarchy would concern itself exclusively with the *quality* of our days. Whither the collective desire to make life better for *everyone*? Ambition is inherently egotistical; it is by definition about being in service of the self. Which has never, not once in the history of humanity (can you tell I've not bothered to read Ayn Rand?) made anyone anywhere "happy."

And anyway, haven't we collectively imbibed sufficient narrative about the perils of success and fame already? Haven't we seen how fame can destroy and corrupt, how ambition and greed are twins? How recognition can pervert and compromise? We're all struggling with our own unique little demon conglomerate, and we all have some good luck and some bad luck. Nobody can tell you how to be happy because being happy is one of those things you figure out *by figuring it out*, no shortcuts. Or maybe you don't figure it out, maybe you never figure it out, but that's on you. Everything worthwhile is a sort of secret, anyway, not to be bought or sold, just rooted out painstakingly in whatever darkness you call home.

I'm searching my old notebooks for one quote in particular. It came flooding back soon after I accepted this hellacious assignment. (I mean, women and ambition!? Too vast and complex. What the hell can possibly be said? Women: be more like men! Lean this way! Lean that way! Lean sideways! Pick a direction and contort yourselves heroically toward it at any cost! Never give in, never surrender! You are entitled to dominate! You owe it to all women! Don't tell us what to do! Hear us roar! I dunno, you guys. I do not know.)

It's a line from an essay by Christine Doza in an anthology called *Listen Up! Voices from the Next Feminist Generation.* I was fortunate enough to take what used to be called Women's Studies in high school, and the anthology was our textbook. Bingo, here it is: "When I was little, I wanted to be the president, a firewoman, a teacher, a cheerleader, and a writer. Now all I want is to be happy. And left alone. And I want to know who I am in the context of a world full of hate and domination."

I'd copied it out in huge, swooping letters.

I find Doza online and message her: *Are you the same Christine Doza who wrote "Bloodlove" in* Listen Up! Voices from the Next Feminist Generation?

I want to include her, let her know how much her essay continues to mean to me, twenty-plus years on. She's not a "famous writer." I can find nothing she's published since that essay. But I want to tell her how forcefully she (still!) resonates when I am asked to formally consider the odious topic of women and ambition. She managed to articulate something difficult, profound, and specific (which is hard and rare), and in so doing, she gave me a gift. A jumping off point. Affirmation. Recognition. Clear-eyed dispatch from further on up the road. Fate brought my eyeballs and her words together, and here we still are.

She never responds. I wonder what her deal is. Whatever.

So maybe my great ambition, such as it is, is to refrain from engagement with systems that purport to tell me what I'm worth compared to anyone else. Maybe my great ambition is to steer clear of systems. Any systems. All systems. (Please Like and Share this essay if you agree!) What I would like to say is: Lean in my hairy Jewish ass.

My mother was one of eight women in the UCLA Law School class of 1965. A lot of professors and students treated them horribly, those eight women, because they were "taking up a space a man could have had." Appalling, right? Except, uh, it's true: my mother did not actually want to be a lawyer. Her parents wanted her to be a lawyer. It was fairly radical of her to become a lawyer. She is badass by nature. But she didn't really want to be a lawyer.

Upon graduation, those eight women got together and decided to just ask interviewing firms outright: *Do you hire women?* Legend has it one honcho stroked his chin thoughtfully and replied, with no apparent maliciousness, "Well, we hired a cripple last year."

She practiced law for about a year before she married my dad and had kids and settled into the kind of furious, bored, soul-eating misery that is the hallmark of thwarted women everywhere, from kitchens and gardens to boardrooms and private jets and absolutely everywhere in-between. To this day, if a stranger at a party asks her what she does, she'll lift her chin in a gesture I intimately recognize as *Don't-Fuck-With-Me*, and say, with cement grit and dirt and bone shard in her voice: "I'm an attorney."

And isn't everything we do, everything we reach for, everything we grab at, each of us in turn, a way of struggling onto that ledge, that mythical resting place on which no one can fuck with us? *Don't Fuck With Me* seems as good a feminist anthem for the 21st century as any.

But the mythical resting place is... mythical. And trying to generalize about ambition is like comparing apples and oranges and bananas and flowers and weeds and dirt and compost and kiwi and kumquat and squash blossoms and tomatoes and annuals and perennials and sunshine and worms.

Wanting to be first in your class is and is not like wanting a Ferrari is and is not like being the first in your family to go to college is and is not like wanting to get into Harvard/Iowa/Yaddo is and is not like wanting to summer on Martha's Vineyard is and is not like wanting to rub elbows with fancy folk at exclusive gatherings is and is not like wanting to shatter a glass ceiling is and is not like wanting to write a lasting work of genius with which no one can quibble. Our contexts are not the same, our struggles are not the same, and so our rebellions and complacencies and conformities and compromises cannot be compared. But the fact remains: whatever impresses you always illuminates your ambition.

Some ambition is banal: Rich spouse. Thigh gap. Gold-buckle shoes. Quilted Chanel. Penthouse. Windowed office. Tony address. Notoriety. Ten thousand followers. A hundred thousand followers. Bestseller list. Editor-in-Chief. Face on billboard. A million dollars. A million followers. There are ways of working toward these things, clear examples of how it can be done. Programs, degrees, seminars, diets, schemes, connections, conferences. Hands to shake, ladders to climb. If you are smart, if you are savvy, who's to stop you? Godspeed and good luck. I hope you get what you want, and when you do, I hope you aren't disappointed.

Remember the famous curse? May you get absolutely everything you want.

Here's what impresses me: Sangfroid. Good health. The ability to float softly with an iron core through Ashtanga primary series. Eye contact. Self-possession. Loyalty. Boundaries. Good posture. Moderation. Restraint. Laugh lines. Gardening. Activism. Originality. Kindness. Self-awareness. Simple food, prepared with love. Style. Hope. Lust. Grace. Aging. Humility. Nurturance. Confrontation. Learning from mistakes. Moving on. Letting go. Forms of practice, in other words. Constant, ongoing work. No endpoint. Not goal-oriented, not gendered. Idiosyncratic. Pretty impossible to monetize.

I mean: What kind of *person* are you? What kind of *craft* have you honed? What is my experience of looking into your *eyes*, of being around you? Are you at home in your body? Can you sit still? Do you make me laugh? Can you give and receive affection? Do you know yourself? How sophisticated is your sense of humor, how finely tuned your understanding of life's absurdities? How thoughtfully do you interact with others? How honest are you with yourself? How do you deal with your various addictive tendencies? How do you face your darkness? How broad and deep is your perspective? How willing are you to be quiet? How do you care for yourself? How do you treat people you deem *unimportant*?

So you're a CEO. So you made a million dollars. So your apartment is photo-ready. So the Times wants to know what you ate for breakfast. So your face is in a magazine. So your song is on the radio. So your book is #1. So you got what you wanted and now you want something else. I mean, good, good, good, great, great, great. You probably worked really hard; I salute you.

But if you have ever spent any time around seriously ambitious people, you know that they are very often some of the unhappiest crazies alive, forever rooting around for more, having a hard time with basics like breathing and eating and sleeping, forever trying to cover some hysterical imagined nakedness.

I get that my foremothers and sisters fought long and hard so that my relationship to ambition could be so… careless. I get that some foremothers and sisters might read me as ungrateful because I don't want to fight their battles, and I don't want to claw my way anywhere. My apologies, foremothers, it's true: I don't want to fight. Oh, is there still sexism in the world? Sigh. Huh. Well. Knock me over with a feather. Now: how do I transplant the peonies to a sunnier spot so they yield more flowers next year or the year after? How do I conquer chapter three of this new novel? I've rewritten it and rewritten it for months. I need to sit quietly for a while. Then some laundry. And the vacuum cleaner needs a new filter. Then respond to some emails from a woman for whom I'm serving as doula.

And it's actually our anniversary, so I'm gonna write my spouse a letter. Then pick up the young'un from school. And I need to figure out what I'm making for dinner. Something with lentils, probably. And butter. Then text my friends a funny photo and talk smack with them for a while.

Taking care of myself and my loved ones feels like meaningful work to me, see? I care about *care*. And I don't *care* if I'm socialized to feel this way, because in point of fact I *do feel this way*. So! I am unavailable for striving today. I'm suuuuuper busy.

Yes, oppression is systemic, I get it, I feel it, I live it, I struggle, I do. Women are not equal, we're not fairly represented, the pie charts are clear as day: nothing's fair, nothing at all, it's maddening, it's saddening, it's not at all gladdening. We all suffer private and public indignities big and small. It's one thing to pause and grapple with unfairness, but if we set up camp there, we can't get much done, can't get to the root of the problem. So sure, great, go on and on about how women should help other women, rah-rah, put it on a T-shirt. Great marketing, but what's actually being accomplished? Who, specifically, is being helped? A collection of egos screaming ME ME ME is not artistically or intellectually or practically productive or interesting.

"Real" work is often invisible, and maybe sort of sacred as such. The hollering and clamoring and status anxiety and PR two inches from our collective eyeballs all day? Not so much. So tell the gatekeepers to shove it, don't play by their rules, and get back to work on whatever it is you hold dear. Nothing's ever been fair. Nothing will ever be fair. But there is ever so much *work* to be done. Pretty please can I go back to my silly sweet secret sacred novel now? Take care.

My little boy is beside me. He is designing cars on BMW's website. Cars are a fleeting obsession. He'd like a BMW someday. His dad and I hide our smirks. Sure, kid, whatever floats your boat. Yesterday it was a Porsche. Tomorrow a Maserati. Apparently he's in an id phase.

"Why don't you guys like fancy cars," he wonders.

"They're a little show-off-y," I say.

"I like fancy cars," he says. "When I grow up I'm going to get a Tesla and a Bentley and a Cadillac and a Rolls Royce."

I smile. "Can I have a ride?"

"Of course!"

Wait, though, there are plenty of material goods I covet. I have a shameful thing for clothes. There's this pair of Comey high waisted pants, oh my god. I own like four pairs of clogs. I live beautifully. Nice textiles, what have you. There's a Kenzo sweater I might be saving up for. I do so enjoy the darkest of chocolates and juice extracted in the most exceptionally newfangled way, I really do.

What I would *like* to say (so that I might be forced to align myself) is that there is nothing material or finite that I will allow myself to *rest* on wanting. Okay, so dresses and clogs and art and peonies float my boat. But fool myself into thinking that these things constitute an end point, or that their acquisition will make me whole, or that people who are impressed by these things are my *friends*? No way. Not for a minute. (Well, FINE, maybe for a minute. But *certainly* not for two.)

Asked for writing advice, Grace Paley once offered this: "Keep a low overhead."

So becoming a lawyer was more or less an exercise in *Don't Fuck With Me*, but what *did* my mother want to do? In her seventies now, she's studying Joyce and Dickens at UCLA and Shakespeare at Oxford. She is delighted and enlivened and occupied, and I wonder aloud why she doesn't go ahead and get herself a graduate degree in Literature. She would make a formidable English professor.

"I'm too old," she says.

"Bullshit," I say.

"I'm stupid," she says. I squint at her.

"I'm lazy," she amends, and my heart breaks for both of us.

She used to tell me *I* was lazy, back when I was refusing to care about my GPA, refusing to run the college admissions race, refusing to duly starve myself like all the good lil' girls at prep school, refusing to wax my asshole or get manicures or chemically straighten my hair, refusing to do much of anything other than consume books and music and movies and books, then scrawl my favorite bits all over the damn place. She was talking to herself all along. She was talking to *herself!* Remember: our most haunting, manipulative ghosts always, always are.

I wrote a magazine piece a while back, and it's been shared online some sixty thousand times. It's an okay piece, but is it the *best* thing I've ever written? I don't think so. Is it the most *original* thing I've ever written? Nah. Is it the most challenging, bold thing I've ever written? Nope.

Sixty thousand shares is not a *win*, see; it's a random, synchronistic event. The number of eyeballs on a given piece of writing does not confer nobility or excellence upon said piece of writing. If the number of eyeballs on a piece of writing excites and impresses people *around* me, that's great, in that it makes possible more of the work I want to do. But it doesn't make said work any easier! And I'm going to do said work regardless, so... what?

So What? Let's add it to our list of proposed feminist anthems: *So The Fuck What?*

You should write for a larger audience, my friend Josh told me a year before he died. He had read my first novel and written to congratulate me. I was on the road, touring, short-tempered. *I am not writing for an audience at all*, I snapped. *I have no control over audience and zero interest in thinking about it.* I could look up our exchange but I don't want to, because I'm sad he's dead and I'm sorry I snapped at him and I want to transcend physics to tell him I love him, and he may be right, and I'm sorry, Josh, and here's a dumb cameo in this dumb essay about dumb ambition.

But I don't *want* to write for a large audience, silly! The masses are kind of mindless as a matter of course, are they not? I mean, no offense, masses, but Trump's memoir sold better than all my past and future work combined. (He didn't *write* it, but still.) The Media Star of the Moment could take a dump on a square of Astroturf and there'd be a line around the block to sniff it. What makes a work of art special and meaningful is your private relationship with it, the magic of finding it amidst the noise and distraction, the magic of letting it speak to you directly. You *found* it, it's *yours*. (This, however, requires the awesome skill of being able to think for yourself in the first place; hardly a given.) Art can change you; it can move and validate and shift and bait and wreck and kindle you in the best way. And others who feel similarly about said work can be your kin. It is not a more-is-better equation.

I repeat: more is not better.

Josh, darling, I don't write because I "want to be a writer." I don't want to be famous and I don't need my ego inflated. I write to make sense of things, to make order from chaos, to make something from nothing. I write to examine my own thinking. I write because what I have found in the writing of others sustains me. Because while I am struggling to live, the writing—a kind of parallel life—helps me along. Because language is my jam. Because I never learned to play guitar and no one ever asked me to sing in a band.

I mean, writing is liberation! Or so I tell students. Flex your muscles! Feel the sun on your face, the wind in your hair! Struggle with your shortcomings. Leave everything out on the field! Do it again tomorrow! What rigor. What joy. Say whatever the hell you want to say, however you most accurately can! Complete and utter freedom. Work.

"The notes for the poem are the only poem," wrote Adrienne Rich. There it is. There's my ambition: Notes.

Oh, but get off your high horse, lady. Fucking relax. You Google yourself on the regular. Whenever you deign to log on to Twitter it's to roll your eyes, sure, but *also*—BE HONEST—to type your name into the search box and see if anyone's talking about you. You don't *even have to* type your name in, BE HONEST: it's already there, in the app's fucking memory! Hypocrite. A nice notification or something can float you for about three minutes; a shit mention somewhere can feel like a slap in the face, even if it's barely literate, even if it's ignorant and hateful and so muddled it's obviously not about *you*. And even as you're skimming it, telling yourself you don't *look at this shit*, you don't care, you don't care, you *are* looking at it, you *are* rooting around in it, you are you are you are you *so are*. Be honest.

The Latin root, by the way, is *ambitio*, which literally means *to go walking*. As in canvassing, as with a political candidate. A friend who's running for city council in New Jersey tells me this. *I am the definition of ambitious,* she says, giggling, because she happens to be one of the most unassuming people I've ever met. She's been going door to door for months leading up to the election. I hope she wins. She would do a magnificent job, and her corner of the world would be better for it. But she's not who I have in mind, here. The root bears little resemblance to the plant that shoots up from it. (Reader, she won!)

Last week a younger writer emailed to ask for advice. How could she get more attention for her book? Where should she send it? The subtext: She wants what (she imagines) I have. It was funny, given that, in truth, I had right at that moment been pouting about my own status (Not Good Enough). I barely know this girl, haven't read her book, she's a bore on social media, but hell, what does it cost me? I wrote back right away.

Send it to writers whose work you admire, I told her. Keep your head down. Do your work. Focus on the work at hand, not the work that's done. Do the work you're called upon to do. Engage with what moves you. Eventually you'll get recognition. And if you *don't* get recognition? Well then, all the more badass to continue working your butt off. Recognition has nothing to do with the work, understand? The work is the endeavor. The work is the process.   Recognition comes, if/when it does, for work that is already done, work that is over. Recognition can really fuck you up. Remember the famous koan? The day before enlightenment, chop wood and carry water; the day after enlightenment, chop wood and carry water. Substitute recognition for enlightenment, putting aside how ironic that is, and there you have it.

It probably wasn't the advice she was hoping for. She never even wrote back to say thanks (tsk tsk, ambitious girl). I thought of her a few days ago, when I heard Ani DiFranco sing "Egos Like Hairdos:" *Everyone loves the underdog, but no one wants to be him...*

Here's what bothers me about ambition, the assumption that we all aspire to the top, the winner's circle, the biggest brightest bestest, the blah blah blah, and that we will run around and around and around our little hamster wheels to get there: most of these goals are standardized. Cartoonish. Cliché. Beware anything standardized, that's what I would teach my daughter. Health care, ambition, education, diet, culture: name it, and you will suffer endlessly from any attempt to go about it the same way as some projected Everyone Else. You cannot be standardized. You are a unique flower, daughter. Maybe the Ivy League will be wonderful for you; maybe it will crush your soul. If the former, I will mortgage the house to pay your way; if the latter, give that shit the finger and help me move these peonies, will you? You are not defined by such things, either way. Anyway, let us discuss what we want to whip up for dinner and take turns playing DJ while doing so.

"She can, though every face should scowl / And every windy quarter howl / Or every bellows burst, be happy still." That was Yeats.

I mean, fuck ambition, that's where this is going. I don't buy the idea that acting like the oppressor is a liberation, personal ambition being, in essence, see above, patriarchal.

And yeah, *about* recognition. What about when genius and/or hard work *isn't* recognized? Because often it isn't, and what do we make of that? And what happens when the striving becomes its' own end? What's been accomplished in such cases? You can get pretty far on striving alone, God knows. The *striving* might get recognized, but what relationship does striving have to mastery? And what's the *cost* of the striving? And what if we confuse striving or incidental recognition *with* mastery? What then!? Then, Jesus, we are so very lost. And we'll have to acknowledge, yes of course sure, that we were born at the right time in the right place and we've never felt bad about working toward what we want, but want is tricky, so beware *that* particular sand trap. Right, and okay, be ambitious, whatever that looks like for you, but don't confuse your own worth with anyone else's definition of success. And don't think that if you happen to impress people you must be very impressive indeed. And don't imagine that if you play by someone else's rules you can win. Anyway, there is no winning. Anyway, the game is suspect. Anyway, write your own rules! Anyway, WHO HAS TIME FOR GAMES!?

"The highway is full of big cars / going nowhere fast / and folks is smoking anything that'll burn / Some people wrap their lives around a cocktail glass / And you sit wondering where you're going to turn." Maya Angelou.

There is a way to spin it so that I am a winner, a success. Go me. Six-figure book deals. Media attention galore. Invitations to read and lecture and teach and reside. Fan letters. Hate mail. Hollywood knock-knock-knockin' at the door. A fossilized nutcase or two trying to take me down.

There is an equally factual way to spin it so that I am a middling mediocre failure, a nonstarter. I've been rejected by plenty of highbrow writer shit. I'm no household name. I don't tweet. I get ignored. You can't find my books at the airport. It just depends on the story you want to tell, the parts to which you are privy. Be assured, my website lists the hits alone.

"The quality I most abhor in women is humility, which seems like a chickenshit response to the demands of the world, or the marketplace, not that I can tell them apart." That's Emily

Carter, who I really wish would publish her second book already.

It hasn't helped that I rarely deign to *apply* for the highbrow writer stuff. Or that when I do, it's in vaguely mocking tones, as sort of an elaborate joke. I'm pretty terrible at applying for things. I should work on that. The snarling girl resents the expectation that she bow down before some purported authority so they might consider throwing her a bone. If they don't want her outright, she doesn't want their farty old bone anyway. Maybe she's not so dormant as I like to think. Or maybe my mother was right: Maybe she *is* just goddamned lazy.

I recently met a writer at a party. The finest MFA, flashy blurbage, all the right everything. I'd heard good things about her first book and told her I was looking forward to reading it.

"Thanks," she said, looking right through me. Our mutual friend said, "Oh my god, have you read Elisa's book? It's so good." The writer could not have been less interested. "What's it called," she wondered in monotone. "You'll have to forgive me, but I really don't keep up with much contemporary writing." The condescension was burlesque. Our friend mentioned the title of my last book, and the light went on in the writer's eyes. Ding. "Oh!" she said. "Oh YES!" Then she looked at me eagerly, hungrily, and I excused myself immediately.

It's creepy, it's actually borderline sinister, that I supposedly "matter" to those kinds of people now, that's all I want to say. That I "matter" *not* because of the books themselves, *not* because of the work therein, *not* because of what prompted the work, *not* because of my *actual humanity*, but because various and sundry radio programs and magazines and newspapers and podcasts and shares and mentions and likes and dings and dongs and film agents and foreign translations and lists *say* I matter. Some supposed authorities have deemed me worthwhile, and so now I "matter." That is, until *these* authorities fade away, only to be replaced by *new* authorities. Gawd, I hope *they* like me. Just kidding. Fuck authority.

Last thought: I wish I had gotten some other lessons from my mother. More about what to make for dinner and how to move the peonies and just how tender and trustworthy love can be, for starters. But we get what we get, so I suppose I appreciate her gift (such as it is) of Don't Fuck With Me. Especially because, have I mentioned? I'm busy channeling it, hard at work. Hashtag blessed. Hashtag grateful. Like? Like??

Last-last thought: I showed a draft of this essay to a trusted advisor. He didn't like it at all. "You sound arrogant," he said. "You're not arrogant, so why are you putting on this front?"

"Ummmm," I said. "Fake it til you make it?"

"You sound like you think you're above all the bullshit, and that's a real turn-off."

"I'm trying to articulate something difficult about art and commerce," I sulked.

"Try and be more vulnerable," he said. "You'll come across better."

Come *across*? I don't have *time* to orchestrate how I *come across*, dude. My job is to write shit *down*. More *vulnerable*? I feel like I'm walking around without *skin* most of the time, *hello*? Anyway, my vulnerability is not for goddamn *sale*. I'd rather suck a thousand dicks.

I was overcome with frustration and weariness, and I thought: *Fuck it, I give up.* But no, that's not true, either. I don't give up. Not remotely. Not at all. The snarling girl is still out there, still in here, flailing, and who's going to throw her a rope?

I will. Onward.

(*Double Bind: Women on Ambition*, W.W. Norton, 2017)

SPRING, ALBANY

THEY POISONED the water in the lake again. It's actually more of an enormous pond. They poison it a few times a year.

I'm not listening to music, for a change. My battery's at 10%, and I want to eavesdrop. The park's full of people. Just like the Seurat painting, minus the class status and pointillism.

There's a black man fishing with his tiny son crouching beside him. The man's biceps are impressively built and inked. The boy says, "Tell me when you see a fish."

There's a middle-aged couple, sort of soul-level beige with a contented aura, walking a mid-sized grey mutt.

There's a petite brown woman in tight blue athleisure berating a man who is pushing a baby in a stroller. Not a status stroller. Athleisure is on the man about something. He hadn't been on time to pick her up. He is playing it cool ("Well, I came, didn't I?"), but she is unrelenting ("Not when you said you would! Not till after you…"), and then they are out of earshot.

There's a young mother from the nearby cult (I'm sorry: Intentional Community), holding a toddler's hand. The Intentional Community manufactures the kind of old-fashioned wooden toys for which my bored mom friends and I go wild. They live and work in a huge brick mansion northwest of the park. There's free literature about their intentionality to be had in a little kiosk at the entrance to their driveway. Books about making peace with death and living in accordance with the laws of nature. When I was a "new" mother, I used to loiter around that kiosk, wondering whether I should join. They wear homemade clothing and raise children communally. I yearn deeply for the latter but I have a quasi-sexual weakness for fashion, and ultimately I'm not much of a joiner. The young mother in her homemade ankle length skirt and bonnet is talking to a man on a bench by the boathouse. He rests one arm on yet another stroller (not status), in which sits a toddler with a delightful head of tight, ombre ringlets.

The man reaches out a hand as I approach.

"Hello!" he says, like we know each other. I don't think we know each other, but I shake his hand.

"How are you?" he wonders.

I smile, nod. "Fine, fine, thank you, and you?" I do this intuitive sort of bow and continue on my way. The cult woman slightly glares at me from under her bonnet. Her glare (Real? Imagined?) trips some anxiety about running into people I'm not fond of, by which I mean people not fond of me. There's this one neighborhood woman in particular, your standard bad-vibes-in-small-town situation; my nervous system goes insane whenever she's nearby.

Officially it's a city of a hundred thousand, but it feels like a small town. Which can make it hard to take a walk sometimes. *Small-bany*, some call it. *Shmalbany*, I prefer. *Albanality*, a friend of mine says, but the syllables don't work. There's not that fantastically freeing anonymity of your big exciting status places. It's a small goddamn town. So much chitchat always needing to be had. Just around that bend? Just over this hill? Just past that tree? I arrange my face in a blank mask and bland smile. I catch myself doing so, catch my thoughts circling this dumb anxiety, shake it off. *You are safe*, I tell myself. It's hard trying to be friends with everyone all the time. It's *okay* if not everybody likes you. Big status city people know this instinctively.

I used to kind of seek out people with bad energy, try to *make* them like me, but that only makes them like you *less*. I learn ever so slowly.

You are safe, I tell myself, and it works. I *am* safe. Relatively speaking. More often now I seek to avoid or minimize encounters with people who don't like me, people who bring out the ugly. This is progress, according to my meditation teacher.

This is the kind of inner drama we all share, right? Useless, banal. Best kept to oneself, only then how are we to take comfort in the knowledge that we're all the same!?

Two white men are sitting on a bench, sharing a joint. One takes a drag, coughs extensively, hocks an impressive loogie.

And there's the official sign, stapled to a tree: PESTICIDE TREATED WATER. On bright yellow laminated paper. The date is filled in, and the illegible name of some pesticide. *Do not swim, 24 hours. Do not drink, 24 hours. Do not fish, 24 hours.*

What happens is, people feed the ducks all manner of processed crap and the ducks shit their brains out and the duck shit throws off the PH balance in the water and the algae flourish and everything's a mess, so: poison.

It's about a mile around the lake (enormous pond? lagoon?), and there's just that one single, solitary sign. The water smells weird, looks weird. Sinister, though maybe I'm projecting. Brackish, with a sort of opalescent film. I don't want to be near it. I move through the cloud of weed smoke near the men on the bench, and detour off the lake path.

Once, in Dolores Park in San Francisco, I came upon two tough-looking teenage girls (but affluent; their shoes gave it away) in a cloud of weed smoke. I asked if they knew where I could get some. It was dusk. I was on a work trip, alone and lonely. Offer me a stupid hit, girls, just offer me one stupid little hit.

"Nope," they said, avoiding eye contact.

"Well, fuck you, too," I muttered as I walked away.

These men, sharing a joint on a park bench in Albany, in broad daylight, would have offered to share, I bet. But then I'd owe them something. Then I'd run into them and they'd know me. Shmalbany.

The ice cream truck's circling the park, trailing its dinky rendition of Scott Joplin's "The Entertainer." Melancholy pang of missing my kid, who's at school. Maybe homeschooling is the way. Maybe I should join the cult. Maybe my quasi-sexual weakness for fashion is holding me back. Maybe we could sit in the park all day eavesdropping and eating ice cream, wearing homemade clothing in a perpetual spring.

I worry for the ice cream truck. Is there enough business? Last year, over Sno-Cones, I asked the driver how it was going.

"Not so good," he said.

I hope the ice-cream truck will be all right. What's a park without an ice-cream truck? It would be just like Shmalbany to fail to sustain a goddamn ice cream truck.

When I was ten, eleven, twelve, living with my mother in a Beverly Hills rental apartment right next to Roxbury Park, there was a great ice cream truck. A thirty-something Iranian ran it. He had a thick, perfect mustache, meticulous comb-over, and melodious accent. He had an eager, unselfconscious grin. He *adored* me for some reason. Whenever I think of him, I am amazed that this story doesn't take a dark turn. No dark turn whatsoever. This man gave me free Big Sticks two, three times a week, and that's not a euphemism. He invited me to sit in his truck and he grinned his enormously kind grin and he told me I was wonderful, beautiful, smart, and good. He told me I could come to his truck anytime I wanted, anytime I wanted I could hang out with him, and he would love it. I wonder if I'm suppressing some memory, here. What are the odds? Reader, that man did not rape me.

My mother was I don't even know what to call it, my oldest brother had gone far away to college, my middle brother had gone to live with friends, and I had no idea where my father was. San Luis Obispo, maybe? Texas? The ice cream man was sort of all I had. And I'm so very sorry to tell you that I ghosted him after a while, because what kind of weirdo would *adore* me? His kindness creeped me the fuck *out*. And that, unfortunately, is more or less how I continued to conduct myself in intimate relations for the following two decades.

I venture up toward the playground, where the slide's still busted. It's been busted for a year. Obviously the city doesn't want to pay for a whole new play structure. They're much too busy widening the highway to better accommodate the bomb trains, which of course run right alongside the projects. Periodically there's a public hearing to voice environmental concerns, but no one outside the projects gives enough of a shit.

There's an orange cone sitting atop the hole in the slide. A dozen tiny kids from the church daycare on Lancaster are exhorted to avoid the cone, the slide. I'll have to write a letter. A series of letters. Who do they think they are, compromising the play of our city's children? Who do they think they are, compromising the air quality of our city's residents? I am outraged.

(*You are safe.*)

(Am I!?)

Albany's a long way from Beverly Hills. What kind of idiot grows up in Beverly Hills and winds up living in Albany!? Might as well be Siberia in the winter. (This idiot.)

This park was conscripted for public use in the city's 1686 charter. Bordered by Madison Avenue (four-lanes, people driving too fast, pathetic few blocks of on-street bike lanes despite ongoing advocacy, lined with make-shift/failing small businesses and the grandest seen-better-days brownstones you can imagine, crosswalks in dire need of repainting), Willett Street (one way, people driving too fast, ditto the brownstones), State Street (same, same), and South Lake (two lanes, *way* too fast, same).

"Academic bride," I tell urbane acquaintances who, with polite, subtle grimaces, wonder *why*. Interesting how many Brooklyn lefties full of self-righteous social media activism wouldn't set *foot* north of Hudson.

PEOPLE LIVE HERE, I occasionally scream at cars going too fast. Call it a hobby. There's a pedestrian-right-of-way on the way into the park from Hudson Ave. It boasts a three-foot-high fluorescent yellow sign that is, more often than not, lying on its side. Last year I wrote to the mayor and the city engineer and our councilman and neighborhood association president, got fifty friends and neighbors to co-sign. Could we please get some speed bumps around the park? (No, because emergency vehicles would be hindered.) Could we please increase signage?

(They'd take this into careful consideration.) Could we please get a ton of reflective road-signs installed? (Maybe!) Could we reduce the speed limit in the park? (Maybe!) *I'm so glad you've chosen to raise your family here,* wrote the mayor in her gracious fuck-off.

Nothing's changed. A state worker advises me to resend the same letter twice a week in perpetuity. This I have not done. I should. I will.

If I'm in a pissy mood and people are blowing through that crosswalk, I sometimes holler *YOU HAVE TO STOP!* Sometimes I even shake my fist.

If I especially don't want to sit at my desk and write, I'll occasionally just saunter slowly back and forth across that crosswalk for a good ten or fifteen minutes, making every. Single. Vehicle. Stop. That's right, fuckheads, the world ain't your goddamn highway. Yesterday I screamed *YOU HAVE TO FUCKING STOP* at a black BMW.

I enjoy my totally ineffective brand of urban-renewal activism.

I should meditate more.

At least Rockefeller didn't manage to build the actual highway *through* the park, like he wanted to. Nelson A. Rockefeller. Can't talk about Albany without talking about that piece of shit. Ashamed of the city's perceived shabbiness (all those "ethnic" neighborhoods!), he decided to transform it, leave his mark, blah blah, eminent domain, blah blah, razed a thousand perfectly good nineteenth century brownstones, destroyed the South End, desiccated the vibrant immigrant communities therein, paved over the trolley tracks, and installed his massive brutalist concrete state capitol complex (which is, admittedly, sort of cool, but if we could turn back time...).

The dumb highway Nelson *did* build blocks pedestrian access to the Hudson River almost entirely: a footbridge can take you from Broadway up and over the dumb highway so you can sit or walk on the bank of the river like a human animal. A single solitary *footbridge.* One footbridge. To connect the homo sapiens of the capital city of New York State to our majestic estuary. In all fairness, the river stank so bad in the sixties that no one wanted to be near it. A poisoned river. Save us from ourselves, Nelson A. Rockefeller! Save us from the stinking river, Pete Seeger!

The year he was five, my kid was really into Pete Seeger. Also, cops. He wore a cop uniform every single day. We had to wash it while he slept. He wrote endless parking tickets and constantly stopped by our local precinct to say hi to "our buddies." He was in a super-ego phase, I suppose. The cops adored my little guy. They showed him around over and over, day in and day out, let him sit in squad cars, flash the lights, run the sirens. They gave him blank tickets and violation slips. (*Not supposed to do this,* they always told me.) They gave him patient, detailed tours of their uniforms. Eventually they even let him hang out in the break room, which meant that I, too, spent a lot of time in local precinct break rooms. I'd bat my lashes: *Thank you so much, guys.* Every day the kid would show up with a thank you note for the day before; soon their walls were covered. He knew their names and ranks. They called out to him from squad cars all over town.

It was the height of Black Lives Matter. Cops were very, very bad. Looming over interstate 90 was a loathsome "Blue Lives Matter" billboard, paid for by the Police Association. Everywhere my kid went in uniform that year, without fail, white people grinned and said, *Thanks for keeping us safe, son!* or *Keep up the good work, kid!* And people of color grinned and said, *Don't arrest me!* or *I didn't do it!* or, most shockingly, *Don't shoot!* I watched these identical scenes play out everywhere we went that year: Albany, Troy, Hudson, Manhattan, Brooklyn, Los Angeles.

One of our neighborhood bike cops worked out of the basement of a flower shop on Lark, don't ask me why. The girl at the counter had a huge black beehive and made these neat rockabilly glitter-and-neon tiki mask paintings.

"Is Kevin around?" my little son would saunter in and casually ask.

"What up, buddy," Kevin would say, emerging from basement stairs carpeted in rose petals. Kevin was an Adonis. Even I was a little obsessed with Kevin.

I asked Kevin and some of the other cops to patrol the pedestrian crosswalk, nail some drivers blowing heedlessly through, and at the end of the summer I bought two tiki paintings from the flower shop girl. Neon green on pink glitter and red on turquoise glitter. They hang above my desk. Tiki masks are said to provide protection and luck. I wanted them in the entry hall or the dining room, maybe, but they freaked my husband out.

Another of the cops who was always so nice to my kid turned up in the news last fall, shortly after Halloween. He had used "excessive force" with a twelve-year-old, and had been temporarily suspended, at which point it was uncovered that he had used excessive force with an elderly man a few years back. So now he was permanently suspended.

I leave the park, walk toward Central Ave, Albany's United Nations. Caribbean deli, Halal butcher, knock-off brand-name street clothes, cell phone stores, Vietnamese place, Chinese noodles, Pakistani food, Kosher vegetarian place (soon to close).

Arty fucks from Hudson are always coming up here to shop at the Asian market, then hightail it back to their fifteen-dollar cocktails and farm-to-table.

Right turn onto Lark, which has seen better days. The denizens of this bus stop in particular seem as good a litmus test as any for the health and sanity of our citizenry. Suffice it to say: seen better days.

The regularity of window-rattling bass is a given. Gangs of choppers, modified sedans. There is sometimes an electric sign warning against noise pollution. The sign comes and goes.

There's Jammella, who works at the espresso place. *Hi, Jammella.* There's "The Mayor," an unhoused guy who washes windows and shovels snow for ten bucks. *Hey, Mayor.* In a few months he'll go bonkers and smash the front window of the crappy dry cleaner for no apparent reason. There's one of the Arab brothers who owns NoHo Pizza. Not to be confused with SoHo Pizza, a few blocks down. *Hey, pizza brother.*

A massive New England banking chain recently ditched their flagship in the grand old savings bank on the corner, and people said this is it, this is really the end of Lark Street. Grim! But soon a church called "New Hope" took over the grand old savings bank, and who could argue with that?

New construction on Lark and Madison, in a long-vacant lot where they once found "historical artifacts" (read: human remains). The ground floor retail has been empty for three years and counting, because they're asking laughably high rent. I'm guessing the developer doesn't live anywhere near here.

For a while I was convinced that Albany's salvation rested on American Apparel opening an outpost in that space. I wrote a letter, suggested they "refine their brand" by setting up shop here. It would be their *only* Hudson Valley/Capital Region store, and didn't they know about what was *happening* in this area? All the Brooklyn hipster refugees and so forth? (Lies!) And wouldn't their brand *profit*, branding-wise, from being the first to colonize this gorgeous, haunted old city, rife with *actual* punks and *actual* ethnic and class diversity and all kinds of folk for whom *not* having to schlep to the godforsaken *mall* to buy underpants would be a true and precious *miracle*? Didn't they like the idea of being *pioneers?* I kept throwing around the word *brand*. Brand! Brand! Brand! Then American Apparel declared bankruptcy and closed all their retail shops all over the world.

I know a woman who waged a successful years-long campaign to bring Trader Joe's to the Capital Region, but of course they opened way over at the intersection of all the highways, big-box territory, near the malls, which they're now talking about turning into big hotels and indoor amusement parks, since a lot of folks have by now caught on to the fact that malls are gross and dumb and driving everywhere sucks in every physical metaphysical economic environmental way.

We have our resident boosters: bloggers, entrepreneurs, local celebrities. For a time, we had a shop with Edison bulbs and air plants (it closed). Now there's another shop with Edison bulbs and air plants (give it six months). We have a couple okay restaurants. Recently a national chain bought out the adorable independent movie theater and now the movies are slightly less interesting, but there's *another* adorable independent theater a mile away showing second runs for *five bucks.* Their popcorn is made with coconut oil! We have a vegan deli and a skateboard shop and a whole *other* park. We have a public pool and we have libraries and we have farmers' markets. We have a bike shop. We have a new, beautiful coffee shop with avocado toast, and the best used bookstore in the world. And we have communities so outrageously marginalized you just have to sit in your car at red lights on your way to the stupid highway built to assault said communities, bearing helpless witness. And lord almighty, do we have strip malls a few miles up in any direction. Every direction. Do we ever. Lord Almighty.

We cheer for the smallest signs of gentrification and boo when those small signs of gentrification fizzle. We invite friends to visit during the spring, summer, or fall. Lilacs in bloom, birds chirping, cobblestones all cobbled, leaves turning. We picnic in the park. We host house parties. We burn wish paper in the fire pit. We run into neighbors, always, always running into neighbors. We watch the sun set on Nelson's stupid / outrageous / terrifying / beautiful Plaza. We gawk at the insane modern art collection in the strange underground tunnel system beneath the plaza, which belongs to us, because Nelson left it all to the citizens of the State of New York.

"Life seems pretty great here," say our status-weary visitors.

"Yeah," we say.

"It could be worse," we add.

"It has potential," we decide.

At the espresso place I run into a "new" mother who just moved here for grad school. She despises it.

"I know," I say. "I totally, totally know. But honestly, all you need is a few good/real friends and it's hard to make good/real friends anywhere." I rattle off hikes, day trips, festivals, happenings, nooks and crannies. It takes time, I tell her, but if you put in the work this place reveals itself to be alright.

I am no longer a "new" mother. I suppose now I'm a "seasoned" mother. Soon enough I'll be an Amazon, a Crone, and I'll joyfully reclaim it in a think piece or ten.

Last fall there was this sweet little house for sale in a swell Berkshires town. I wanted to move. *Let's get out of here,* I whined. Having traded the dank one-bedroom in Brooklyn for this grand Albany townhouse, we could now trade the grand Albany townhouse for a pastoral cottage within walking distance to a (presumably non-poisoned, or as non-poisoned as anything is anymore) lake and sweet town at the foot of a mountain half an hour from any highway.

We didn't do it.

One of my students tells me the indigenous people avoided Albany, claiming that this place has circular energy. It could trap you, keep you.

I continue holding forth for the "new" mother on the excellent local street art: the black-and-white bicyclist on the corner of Henry Johnson and Washington! The stunning elk in the parking lot between Spring St. and Washington! The Bluebirds commissioned by the city on the side of a concrete parking garage facing the highway on the river! The head of Rockefeller assaulted by a Sven Lukin piece way downtown. (*People come to take pictures all the time*, said the man on the stoop of the dilapidated row house next door when I stopped to take a picture.)

Oh, and had she been to Troy? Troy is cool. Troy: forget about it. Troy is so cool it is almost too late for Troy. Get your real estate while the gettin's good! Or no, wait, actually: don't!

I wander over to the used bookstore in search of Paula Fox's *Desperate Characters*, which I score, alongside Wollstonecraft's *A Vindication of the Rights of Woman*, Philip K Dick's *Do Androids Dream of Electric Sheep?*, Montaigne's *Complete Essays*, and Lethem's *You Don't Love Me Yet*. I spend a grand total of nineteen dollars on this haul.

My family of origin still lives in West L.A., and I suspect they're a little embarrassed by my living here. Al-bay-nee, they call it. But then again, my mother still refuses to learn how to spell my husband's and son's last name, so maybe it's just constitutional incapacity.

Time to get in the car to pick the kid up from school. Driving is my least favorite. Once home again, we have a snack and ride bikes into the park. We dismount at the pedestrian crosswalk, because, as I always tell him, cars are big idiot asshole monsters and want to kill you. The boy has learned to hold up his hand in a STOP gesture, wait for oncoming cars to stop, then cross.

"Let's see if people are gonna be assholes today," he says. No idea where he picked up that line.

They are not assholes today. He waves to drivers as he crosses, and shouts "Thank you!" They wave back, beaming, then gun their engines and burn rubber.

Later, on the way back from the playground, we stop in our tracks when we hear the tinkling of "The Entertainer." Ice cream truck! Heading this way! The tinkling gets louder, and we see the truck approach. Kid gallops toward it, waving his arms maniacally.

"If you get hit by a car I'll *kill* you!" I holler. But even the briefest imagining of that makes me fucking nauseous, and I'm immediately on the verge of tears (see also: nervous system), worrying that if he *does* ever get hit by a car (GOD FORBID) his last thought might be worry that I'm going to be *mad* at him, and how horrible *that* would be. This is what it's like to be a mother.

Time to meditate some more.

"Hey! Hey! Ice cream truck!! HEY! HEY!!"

We're on a patch of grass by the road, jumping up and down, hands in the air. But the truck doesn't see us, doesn't stop. We watch it speed right through the crosswalk. Asshole must be going fifty miles an hour.

(Longreads, 2016)

EARLY AUTOBIOGRAPHY VIA PROXIMITY TO FAME, OR WHEN PEOPLE ASK WHAT IT WAS LIKE GROWING UP IN L.A.

THE GUY who played Ross on *Friends* grew up next door. His parents were lawyers who swore the property values couldn't get any higher, so they sold too soon. Veronica Hamel, who starred on *Hill Street Blues*, bought our house when we moved. My middle brother's nursery school classmates included Gwyneth Paltrow and Maya Rudolph. His best friend in grade school was Guy Oseary, who went on to manage Madonna and U2. A friend of that brother's from high school went on to a role in a TV show, but I always forget the guy's name. The show was *Suits*, co-starring Meghan Markle, aka Her Royal Highness the Duchess of Sussex.

The Marciano family, who owned *Guess?*, lived on our block in the flats of Beverly Hills in the 80s. The Marciano kids were all cool and nice and everyone rode skateboards and I remember walking around the neighborhood in gangs all the time, in and out of one another's houses. The flats of Beverly Hills in the 80s were weirdly utopian. I was terrible at skateboarding, but I never got badly hurt. A bunch of us were obsessed with the little green buds on Impatiens bushes you could pop with gentle pressure so that they exploded with seeds. "Poppers," we called them, and spent hours roaming the streets in search of them. Or maybe that was just me.

Ariel Rosenberg was in my class at Jewish day school; he

grew up to become musician Ariel Pink, most famous now for having attended the January 6th seditious riot. Elisa Boren, also in our class, was known as Elisa B (I was Elisa A). She was a sweetheart. She married the guitarist of a band called Linkin Park, which I hear is bad.

I wrote a fan letter to Judy Blume; she sent me a form letter in response.

My father dated a woman who was "best friends" with Jane Fonda, and we went to the premiere of some movie Fonda was in, and I was sucking on a Tootsie Pop and Fonda laughed and said, "Now *that's* the way to come to a movie premiere: with a lollipop!" and I liked her a whole lot. I was eleven.

I wrote a fan letter to Patti LuPone; she sent me a signed headshot in return.

I wrote a fan letter to Carol Burnett; she didn't respond. I must have had a thing for redheads. My aunt was a (fake) redhead. My aunt was also a semi-secret lesbian and everyone made fun of her all the time. In my family it was open season on lesbians, fat people, and people without children.

Tori Spelling was a senior when I was a seventh grader at an exclusive all-girls school. She had the best collection of whimsical boxer shorts, which everyone wore under tailored uniform miniskirts. She was very sweet and guileless, it seemed to me, but even then I knew she'd look better if she just let her hair be its natural color and texture.

My father's girlfriend's daughter had a walk-on part on *Beverly Hills, 90210*, in the Very Special episode where a kid accidentally kills himself whilst playing with a gun. She also had a walk-on in the Doors movie starring Val Kilmer. I worshipped her. Eventually her mom and my dad broke up and I never saw or heard from her again and I was sad about it for years. Then one day I found her on Facebook and it appeared she had turned out to be highly basic after all, complete with chemically straightened hair and pseudo-glam shot, so I was finally cured of those particular feelings of loss.

An elderly former actress lived next door to my grandma in an apartment complex in Sherman Oaks. I was *Gone with the Wind* obsessed and got my hands on a cheesy mass-market paperback entitled *Gable's Women*, about the many women Clark Gable romanced. I carried that book with me everywhere, loved reading about Gable's sex life. So here's a strange coincidence: the elderly former actress who lived next door to my grandma turned out to be one of Gable's former paramours! Her name was Virginia Grey. Her headshot from 1943 was featured in the middle of *Gable's Women*. Grandma invited her over to have tea. She was thin and stern and beautiful and elegant and dignified and palsied. She wore a black turtleneck with a string of cinnabar and amber beads. She had grown up in Hollywood. One of her babysitters had been a young Gloria Swanson. Wikipedia says she was featured in over 100 movies from the '30s through the '80s. She was under contract to MGM. She died in 2004 at the Motion Picture and Television Retirement Community in Woodland Hills, and her ashes were scattered at sea.

I gained admittance to a Jewish performing arts troupe when I was thirteen. We went all around town doing original variety shows at synagogues. It felt very professional and ludicrously exciting. When I was younger, I had seen one of their shows and thought this troupe was the most legendarily awesome thing I had ever been near. One of their ballads, based on Hebrew liturgy, reliably moved me to tears. A cute girl from this troupe wound up starring on a Nickelodeon show called *All That*.

Ira Newborn, who did the soundtracks to all my most beloved John Hughes' films, lived around the corner from my mom and went to her shul. He was probably in his fifties then, and single, and looking for someone with whom he might start a family. I was in awe of him because he had masterminded the sonic genius of *Sixteen Candles*, and I was newly of childbearing age, and I wondered if, because he seemed friendly and nice and interested in talking to me at Shabbos dinners, I might be a wife candidate. Surely there were worse fates than living in Brentwood and bearing children for a musical genius. Everyone was always telling me I was mature for my age.

Frank Sinatra had some kind of medical event and collapsed onstage during a concert in Vegas. I was hanging out at a frozen yogurt place in the valley with some of my Jewish performing arts friends, and along came a CBS news crew, doing a man-on-the-street thing. The CBS guy asked: *Do you know who Frank Sinatra is?*

Of course, I said. *Ol' Blue Eyes!*

I was sixteen. They used that clip on the next day's news.

My mother chauffeured me to lots of doctors' appointments because there was a lot allegedly wrong with me. My complexion wasn't wonderful, for one. The dermatologist was nice enough, though he saw fit to put me on a horrific acne drug, which has since been shown to actually alter DNA, and I had to take the birth control pill alongside it, despite being not remotely sexually active, because it could warp fetuses in the most extraordinary ways. In hindsight, an interesting course of treatment for an otherwise perfectly healthy teenaged girl. This same doctor treated Michael Jackson for vitiligo, and his receptionist, Debbie Rowe, became egg donor and surrogate for Jackson's children.

Steven Spielberg's stepdaughter was two grades ahead of me. Maggie Gyllenhaal was one grade ahead of me. Jake Gyllenhaal was one grade behind me. Jason Segel, too, but he wasn't famous yet. We played mother and son in an Edward Albee play. Also at school: the sons of Neil Diamond and Randy Newman. I had a crush on the son of Randy Newman, but didn't really know who Randy Newman was. I had crushes on a lot of people. I don't think anyone had a crush on me.

Maggie G came to my house for a party. A lot of cool people were at my house that night, and I got stinking drunk because I was freaking out about all the cool people being at my house. Toward the end of the night, I found myself alone in the fetal position on my bedroom floor, in the dark. The door opened and Maggie came in to check on me. No, just kidding, she only wanted to use my phone. She flipped on the light switch, stepped over me, stretched out on my bed, and called her mom to relay a litany of boyfriend troubles while I remained in the fetal position on the floor. When she was done talking on the phone she got up, looked in the mirror for a while, stepped back over me, turned off the lights, and exited the room.

I was going to play Adelaide in *Guys and Dolls* senior year. I was going to hit it out of the park. But I didn't get the part. The drama teacher was very into *his* proximity to celebrity, so he cast all his shows with names. Tyrone Power's granddaughter got Adelaide. Tyrone Power's granddaughter didn't even seem that interested in theater! Rumor had it she had been coerced by the drama teacher into auditioning! Plus her voice kinda sucked! I was way pissed. I had *crushed* "Adelaide's Lament" in tryouts. I wrote an anonymous letter to the school newspaper, critiquing the drama teacher's methodology/starfucking. It caused quite a stir. Everyone knew I had written the letter.

I saw Al Pacino out in Santa Monica somewhere one night. Coffee Bean and Tea Leaf, I want to say it was. He was smoking. I casually asked if I could bum a cigarette. He stared at me with great intensity, did not move a muscle in his face, pulled a single cig from his pack of Camel Lights, and extended it out to me, all without saying a word or breaking gaze. I said thanks, then bolted. I put that cig into a Ziploc baggie and pinned it to my bulletin board and occasionally fondled it for a long time thereafter. A decade went by before I finally smoked it, out my old bathroom window, on a visit home. It was stale.

I was carted off to a couple different psychologists. One of these was a rather underwhelming lady who some years later was named in all the gossip rags for having been the one to commit Britney Spears to an involuntary stay at a mental hospital after a forty-five minute consultation.

Prom night a group of us had a suite at the Sunset Tower hotel. Down the hall was Dave Gahan from Depeche Mode and he wound up in our suite, wanting to "party" with us. I recall his ghostly pallor and sunken eyes and greasy hair. He was talking a mile a minute. I didn't know who he was. Later that night he OD'd down the hall. We found out about it the next day. He lived.

The son of the guy who founded Noah's Bagels was in my year at Brandeis. I was fat and possibly a lesbian and one of my brothers died and everyone told me how fat I was at his funeral (in the cemetery where Al Jolson is buried [h/t Amy Hempel], and Dinah Shore, and Max Ritvo now, too, out by LAX), and I was pretty sure I was at least partly lesbian, and I knew that being fat plus being even a smidge lesbian meant I should probably just kill myself ASAP, so it was interesting to just, like, sit with that.

I sat next to Grace Paley at dinner after a reading. The professor who'd brought her to campus believed in my writing, and seated me with Paley, who was very old and very shrunken and utterly without pretension. She chewed her food like a working-class girl from the Bronx. I loved her profoundly.

That summer I worked in the mailroom at the William Morris Agency. My mom's friend's father had once been head of the agency. Everyone who works at William Morris had to start in the mailroom, per the decree of the founders, so that everyone who rises through the ranks has a foundational understanding of its bottom-up workings. The agents-to-be were vaguely condescending, slick young men in suits. It was the dispatcher I loved. Beefy, soft-spoken guy, amused by the goings on around him, not on his way up, satisfied with his lot: a lifer. When everyone else was out on mail runs, I'd sit on his lap, and we'd get all flushed and giggly.

I almost went to Israel to work in the Jewish Peace Corps after college, agonized throughout the majority of that year's notebook about whether or not I should go to the Middle East and be Of Service, but I said fuck it and moved to New York instead, to work some shitty jobs and Become A Writer, at which point my proximity to fame and fortune positively exploded, to the extent that I became permanently jaded, finding it absolutely pathetic, to say nothing of existentially crushing and spiritually bereft and morally suspect, when people even subtly angle toward fame, or attempt to name drop for any reason at all, in any context whatsoever. So! The end.

(Bennington Review, 2020)

CURRENCY

1.

MAYBE YOU'LL BE AN ACTRESS. Maybe you'll do stand up. Maybe you'll suck dick for money. Maybe you'll wear intense glasses and make dramatic proclamations into a swank office telephone. Maybe you'll meet your married lover for a drink on a rainy night wearing nothing under a coat. Maybe you'll make art in an airy loft in a deserted part of town. Surely there'll be long ruminative walks through the park. The voice-over will be witty as hell.

You can be weird in New York, that much is certain. You can be strange and melancholy and buxom and tall and dark and discerning. You can behave generally like the exuberant nerd bitch dyke intellectual you semi-consciously understand yourself to be. Apparently they value that sort of thing there!

Ape the hell out of Didion's prose in conversing with Dear Diary and get into a decent college despite your hilariously low GPA. Damn, her sentences are cool. Mr. Bellon's AP English class is the only thing about which you can muster a shit to give.

Let's go down to the East River and throw something in, Ani growls over the din of your mother's tirades outside your locked bedroom door. *Something we can't live without and then let's start again.* Mutter this phrase tunelessly while you ride out panic attacks in the shower. Soon you'll be *there* and here won't matter so much anymore.

It won't be Didion's New York, though. Not Woody's, either, or Ani's or Ephron's or Lebowitz's or Sontag's or Warhol's. Not Holofcener's, not Lethem's, not Patti Smith's. Silly—though tempting—to pretend otherwise.

You're neither spoiled nor reckless enough to inhabit the extremes of the experience, but do what you can. Get regularly shit-faced with a gaggle of girls more or less just like you. Give spike heels a try. Take strangers home from bars. (Keep a running list of their names, the names in fact of every man with whom you ever so much as make out.) Rarely turn down an invitation or a narcotic. Wind up in strange / desperate / squalid / exorbitant apartments, clubs, bars, restaurants. Forget how you got there. Guzzle Jack-and-cokes until everyone seems like a dear friend you'll meet again in another lifetime. Bring the house down at Marie's Crisis Café with a deeply felt rendition of "Dance: Ten; Looks: Three."

Flatiron office job, Midtown office job, Gramercy office job, Chelsea freelance job. Forever late to work. One boss gives you a wool and silk embroidered robe from ABC, which decades later turns out to still be one of the nicer things you own. The 2nd Avenue Deli, Veniero's, Tompkins Square on the verge of sanity. Grey Dog Coffee, where your first husband gets himself banned for general orneriness. City Bakery. Community garden on Avenue D. St. Mark's. LifeThyme Natural Foods, Cobble Hill Theater, Yoga Lab, the Victory, Flying Saucer, Blue Sky Bakery. Read the *Post* and the *Daily News* cover to cover over lunch. New York has people, other people, always more and more people. Get to know as many of them as you possibly can. Don't bother to remember bars; bars are interchangeable. Oh, but the Other Room. Oh, but Max Fish. Dress in costume. The laundromat is a treat. Anytime you can walk the streets. Not like in L.A., where life unfolded in the car or at home or in the car or at school or in the car or in the locked bedroom or in the car or at the mall or in the car. Barf, L.A., where girls competed to see who could stand out *least,* who could come closest to disappearing. Your whole childhood boiled down to eating a surreptitious ice cream cone with your face in a book in the backseat of a car driven by a raving lunatic. Yep, ice cream and books got you through, and the books all pointed in the general direction of New York.

At Lil' Frankie's on Fridays, the hot waiter picks up the tab and shares the last bottle with you and your bestie. She thinks he wants her but you're pretty sure he wants you. It's a flirt-off. He wants you both, obviously, but you have zero desire for her. Some other girl eventually sleeps with him. Years later she informs you gleefully, like she won.

Orthodox roommates in doorman rental on West 96th. Railroad shithole with appalling broker's fee on East 11th. Nesting pigeons cooing in the air shaft day and night. Boyfriend's squat on Carmine. Transient girlfriend in a garret (a garret!) down on the Hudson. Amazing below-market brownstone floor-through on Washington Place. Host big parties. Your favorite college professor comes to crash. Fight with the first husband constantly until upstairs neighbors complain about the noise.

Warren Street sublet. State Street gem. Fifth floor walkup with super in VFW cap forever smoking on the stoop. F train, A train, 2 train, 6 train. Bodega, bodega, bodega. Amazing consignment shop on Atlantic. Brooklyn promenade.

On rooftop in Brooklyn at one in the morning PJ Harvey sings about being on a rooftop in Brooklyn at one in the morning, and someone says something you've never forgotten.

Your story's not seldom told, sweetheart.

A summer spent stoned, Dean Wareham flooding the headphones. Cry constantly. Became a student of yoga. Lose friends. Write your way out. Write your way in. Filthy cliché. Fall in love, out, back in. Let a love or two pass you by, so you have something to think about wistfully in old age. Stop drinking, mostly. Give birth in the bathtub of a condo on the fourth floor of the old Board of Education building on Livingston Street. Gather up your fledgling family and flee.

2.

What happened was a wildly great guy. A love affair. Destiny. No idea where Albany was, but you were game. Then the baby, and the living-in-two-places thing got old immediately. You could've fought to stay in the city. But you didn't have a whole lot of fight in you just then, and it was easy to say fuck the city. Felt pretty good, actually. Fuck Brooklyn. Fuck the scene and all who flock to it.

But the harsh reality of Albany. There was some idea that it'd be a friendly place, an instant-community kind of place, because people have to stick together, even more so in a post-industrial wasteland kind of place, right?

No.

A town designed (rather, corrupted; see William Kennedy's "Everything Everybody Ever Wanted" in the definitive *O Albany!*) to discourage human contact, communal life, organic gathering places. Your basic urban-planning nightmare American state capital. Pathetic monument to the personal automobile. The highway blocks direct human access to the river. To reinvent Sinatra: If you can love it here, you can love it anywhere.

At first you get off on going to the mall. After a decade in the Center of The Universe, a cheese-ball suburban mall seems the height of exoticism and delight. Classic beige sterile trying-too-hard fifteen plants in an atrium under a skylight of which some third-rate architect was very proud. State-of-the-art twenty years ago multiplex with arcade. Escalators, muzak, teenagers up to no good. Israelis accosting you with samples of Dead Sea shit from a cart. The hideous seasonal store: Halloween crap, Christmas crap, Valentine's crap, St. Patrick's crap, Easter crap, Fourth of July crap, Back to School crap, and around again.

People in the city cock their heads and say: *How is it up there? Is it, like, really, really cold up there?* Don't blame them; you couldn't find it on a map two years ago, either.

A film buff tells you early noir films were often set in Albany, which adds a nice new dimension. Live alongside an

Olmstead-inspired park, in a grand, creaky old house built around the time your great-great-grandmother was keeping house in some muddy shtetl. Fireplaces, oak moldings, tile bathroom, original tub. Stoop with pale pink columns. Wild, mature perennial garden. When people visit from the city their jaws hang open.

Albany consolation prize, you explain, because it costs roughly the same as a windowless cell in the basement of a house in Crown Heights.

One time you and the kid get caught in a summer downpour on your way home from the park and a lady sees you from her stoop across the street and calls you over to her house, where she makes you tea and gives the kid toys and insists you stay for dinner. The struggling local businesses on bedraggled yet faintly charming Lark Street, forever On the Verge. At LarkFest, drunk dudes urinate and puke everywhere and neighbors commiserate and it's almost cute. Metroland, the highly lovable doomed alternative news weekly. Perpetual fryer smell from Bombers, where you eat once and vow never again, the pristine haven of Crisan Bakery, everything made from scratch by Iggy and Claudia. Dove and Hudson used bookshop: walk in and breathe books and something you've been thinking about—say, Mircea Eliade, say, Mary Daly, say, a guide to Ayurveda—invariably appears on a shelf at eye level. They keep your honey's book in the window, next to the Robert Caro doorstop about Robert Moses, proud of the neighborhood guy done good. Ben and Jerry's on the corner, across from the enormously fat cats at the bodega.

Hi kitty cats, waves your boy as he strollers then trikes then scooters on by.

A spring then summer then fall then winter.

Little guy's growing too fast, says the pockmarked guy who stands out front smoking, keeping watch.

A couple opens an organic local café/bakery on Delaware, down from the Spectrum and New World Bistro. She was crying once when you went in and you understood their undertaking to be unimaginably difficult; traveling to Phish shows in the yellow VW van used to be way more fun than convincing this struggling shit-balls community to rally around its local organic café.

Takes time but you find truly wonderful people. No worries about where the kid will "get in" to preschool. A shaggy collection of salt-of-the-earth people. There's always room for you and your laptop at the okay coffee roaster.

From your kitchen window watch the sun rise on Empire Plaza, Rockefeller's misguided monument to his prick, with its impressive collection of modern art, reflecting pool, neo-fascist concrete expanse, bizarre underground city, wintertime skating rink. The way those four capital buildings stand sentinel on the horizon. The aptly named Egg, where Rickie Lee Jones opens with "Satellites" in the hundred-seat theater.

The drive on 90 to preschool, past Nipper the dog, the hills and the river and the skies you would not believe. Miles and miles of neglected bike path. The U-Haul truck rotating slowly on top of a storage facility on the river.

At the Shitty Bagel Chain surrounded by Real People (meaning: not living meta-lives on top of actual lives, not trained in matters of ultimate coolness, not wealthy, not angling for notoriety), notice how it's a bit less noisy in a super-ego sense. You can relax. You have nothing to prove. Think about an inward-focused life. Where can you best lead one? Do your thing, stand tall. Life's a turning inward, you're convinced lately, a getting quiet, learning to observe and be still. Some call it meditation but you get scared off when it has a name.

Within an hour radius: Troy's vibrancy. Too many kick-ass farmer's markets to count, Saratoga, Hudson, the Berkshires, the Catskills, Ghent, Chatham, Great Barrington, Saugerties, Tanglewood, Mass Moca, Kripalu. You actually love it here, turns out. Look closely: it's a promising place. There's work to be done. There's potential. Put your money and effort and energy *here*, where it's possible to make a difference, make a dent.

What about those creepy bird calls in the train station garage? They sound like rhesus monkeys. What are they? No one seems to know. Detailed conversations between those animals. Turns out they're not animals at all; only a recording designed to discourage *actual* animals from nesting. It's so weird and uncool here, so devoid of cool, that it turns out to be pretty cool. But the question remains, only partially because of the mindfuck of having recently become someone's mother: who the hell are you and what the hell are you doing here?

The question is: Where do you belong?

"Where do you feel taller?" asks a tarot queen on a perfect October day. Excellent question. Up here, you guess. There's your answer, then.

Growing up you loathed being tall. Girls were not supposed to be tall. Girls were supposed to be as small as possible in every conceivable way.

"Where upstate do you live?" wonders a cool girl behind the counter of a cool north Brooklyn café.

"Hudson," you tell her, because you can't deal with this chick writing you off as some irrelevant bumblefuck *mom*. Hudson has name recognition; artists and art and currency. A juvenile need for this random chick to understand that You Are Culturally Relevant. Shame, rage. You're ridiculous. Why this need? Are you *twelve*?

"Oh my god I love it up there!" she says. "Sooooo cool."

You nod. You are an arbiter, goddamn it! AN ARBITER.

3.

To talk about New York City—living there, aspiring to live there, having lived there—is to talk about currency. Not privilege, mind you, and not money. Money is simple. Money is straightforward. Money can give you choices, options, ease. Privilege skews how you see yourself and others, fucks with your perspective. Currency is something else. Currency is terrifically complex. You can't buy currency; it eludes plenty of rich, entitled people. Money and privilege can make you comfortable, but only currency gives you real power.

Beauty, originality, fearlessness: these are a few of the currencies of New York.

Papa Irwin, small time shyster genius youngest son of alcoholic Montreal policeman, bought a parcel of land in Los Angeles on the corner of what is now Sunset and La Brea in 1950, and moved his young family west. Rumor has it he and his uncle were traveling salesmen, sold condoms to whorehouses. Papa called New York City "that cesspool," aghast that you lived there. Alone, no less!

Your parents got married at the hotel from *Pretty Woman*. Big Spanish-style Brentwood homes, Bullocks Wilshire, I. Magnin, sweet sixteen at Louise's. Birds of Paradise, Magnolias, Palms. The flats of Beverly Hills before the Persians arrived. Bat Mitzvah a few blocks from the Santa Monica beach. Fancy private school.

It's not until you're long gone that you begin to understand: it's unusual to be "from" a place that comprises a lot of fantasies. But from there you are, and what an education you got! The culture of name-dropping and status anxiety, the whiff of desperation inherent in any attempt to assert oneself that way: it was in your microwaved baby formula.

You don't seem like you're from L.A., people say.

Thank you, you say.

New York was an escape. You could give a shit about yeah so were having brunch at Balthazar when I blew this marginally famous person in the bathroom of that bar on Ludlow the night of the Williamsburg heroin orgy wearing the dress I bought at the Barney's warehouse sale to the best show ever at the venue on the cover of *Time Out*. All that puff-out-your-chest to prove just how connected and prescient and rooted you are. When obviously the real questions are: who lives in the shittiest neighborhood and cares the least? Who gets in free? Whose art is so essential it cannot be ignored?

Love letters to New York are invariably designed to make the reader feel like a loser. You might feel powerless in New York, but you can always make some shmuck who's never lived there, or better yet *only recently just moved there*, feel even more powerless. Fine: so maybe you remember when Alphabet City was scary and Brooklyn was cheap. Maybe you went to Elaine's, KGB, Mars Bar. Maybe you got mugged. Congratulations. If you remember its previous incarnation, or the incarnation prior to that, you own New York. Here's your I HEART NYC t-shirt. You're legit. You're rooted. Now shush. An ultimately boring ass economics, and honestly the whole marketplace can pretty much suck it.

Your identity isn't reliant on that place, on any place; it's just a construction. Magical thinking. You have Stockholm syndrome: the city took you captive, stole your heart, ran off with your imagination, left you broke and battered. Sure, sing it a freakin' love song. But make no mistake: the city owns you.

Still, you really miss that place, something about its weird, destructive pull. Plenty of good reasons to hop a train down: gigs, friends, family, marvelous head shrinker. Get on the southbound, read a silly rag, watch the river whiz by. Usually a whole row all to yourself. The conductors smile. Mustachioed flat top guy and buxom grandma-type are your favorites. Once in a while the vibe's a little on the scary side. Once there were bomb sniffing dogs and TSA agents. And compared to the train situation in, say, Western Europe, Amtrak is an overpriced disgrace. But it's a lovely liminal space, the train. Put on headphones. More often than not a little stoned. (Only backfires when you miss your train; once you had to drive to Poughkeepsie to catch MetroNorth absolutely baked and your friend stayed on the phone with you the whole way, and you said out loud to her and to yourself and to the empty highway *Okay this is really not okay I'm being an asshole and I gotta cool it with the weed.*) Gather up your stuff at Penn Station. Sentimental souls need rituals. Go up a few escalators and emerge across from the grand steps of the post office on Eighth Ave, where the camera would pan up in a dizzying spiral, if there were a camera.

Paying respects to lost youth, you text people. *Drink?* You hate making plans in advance. You also hate alcohol, but want that looseness you used to enjoy, that who-knows-where-the-night-might-take-you lately in such short supply.

Needless to say, you love your new family. You are awash in love and gratitude for your beautiful life up the river. But you cherish these field trips. Time is not linear. The old you is a fossil trapped in amber, perfectly preserved. Stay in a friend's tiny studio. Read a good book over breakfast at the perfect tiny brasserie down the street.

Sit on your old stoop for a while. Couple hours before the train home. The girls are all in costume. An old lady shuffles past, looking at you, amused. You're in costume, too: city drag. Scribbling in a notebook, to boot. Two women walk by. One is pushing an infant in a stroller, the other's hugely pregnant. The pregnant one says she feels "a lot of pressure." The other one says something-something "heavy." If you're not immersed in such things they can seem repetitive and boring. But if you are immersed in them, they comprise your life, so what are you supposed to do? You waddled these streets with friends, talking about bodies and birth and pressure and heaviness. It now seems an almost unbearably special time, but it was just life.

A film guy and his actress girlfriend moved in when you left. What if they find you sitting here on their stoop? That would be kind of sad. You once ran into the actress around the corner and were embarrassed, like she'd know you were casing her apartment. You're upset they live here, kind of. This magic gem of an apartment that used to be yours. They still get mail for you occasionally. The super died last year. Never saw him smile but he was a good guy. The way he sat there, smoking, vacant stare. The way he said *yeahhhhhh* with that sandpaper voice.

All accountable, reasonably happy grownups are the same, but unhappy immature drama-queen wretches are all unhappy in their own way. There's something terrifically sad about growing up, which is why sometimes people refuse to do it. (Some of your very favorite people.) It's only a place. It isn't responsible for who you've become; it could have been Tel Aviv or Berlin or San Francisco or London. Could've been rural Idaho, Sebastopol, Ireland, Texas. And anyway: how many people are lucky enough to *choose where they live*?

You fell in love here a lot, wrote some books, gave birth. How could that time not hold you in thrall? *Change is seen as something evil only by those who have lost their youth or sense of humor.* That was Cookie Mueller on the East Village, 1985. The city's not the same and you're not the same and you'll never get that time back because time is a spiral, girl: a spiral. Life is elsewhere now. Live it.

It's just you miss the reckless girl who lived here. Retarded funny stubborn blind unforgiving little wench, beholden to no one, blindly enacting her will on everything, everyone. It was your youth! Now you're older and wiser and better in about a thousand ways. A halfway decent sense of self on a good day, for starters. Now you know some things about where to put your energy, about what it means to build up instead of tear down, what it's like to nurture good things so they grow. You wouldn't trade anything for anything. All of this is true. Yet let us not skirt the issue that something was lost. Something has been lost.

(*Goodbye to All That: Writers On Loving and Leaving New York*, Seal Press, 2013)

WHERE I WRITE

OFFICE AT HOME

Set up your office and get to work, a friend instructed a few years back, when I complained about the stalled novel, which had plateaued at halfway done and was thereafter just sitting there. I half-heartedly poked at it a few times a week, but momentum was gone. So I laid down an old Ikea kilim, cleared out clutter, hung pink string lights and cute scrap flags someone sewed me as a gift, and a photograph of a feral house in Detroit (which has a thing or two in common with down-town Albany). Suspended some tillandsia with twine. Now I had a nice quiet little room in which to sit and contemplate the stalled novel.

Just doing the work is the whole battle. "Making contact." Sit with the novel, be in it. Turn off the internet so you have nowhere else to go. Only rarely is it satisfying. Rarely is there a great chunk you can point to at the end of a day: here is what I did today! More often there's the vague fear you've made no progress at all. Where did those hours go? Where is your work? What is this adding up to? You have paid someone else to be with your precious child while you did *this* bullshit? The thing continues and continues to feel like a wreck. But it's *your* wreck. And you *are* working on it, even when it seems like bullshit, eating your time and appearing none the better. *No effort is wasted*, says the Bhagavad Gita on a post-it stuck to the bottom of my giant computer monitor. But God, some days are a slog.

Leaning against doorjamb while boy plays in the bath

The battery on the old laptop is shot. I've got fifteen, twenty minutes, max. Less if I start up iTunes. Fucking machine. It gets hot and gives me a headache. But fifteen minutes is about the length of the bath, so it works out.

Little over five years old, the machine. The boy's a little under five years old. The machine arrived just before the boy. When it wouldn't start the other day I marched it dutifully to the Apple store in the heinous mall, where I was told by a sweet young lady that they would not be able to service it.

"It's a vintage machine," she explained.

"It's five years old," I said.

She nodded at me slowly.

There must be a better way. Pen? Paper?

The boy will be five soon. He still seems pretty little, but maybe it's because the novel is about early motherhood, the desperate combat-zone-like surreality of it. It still takes my breath away, how scared I was. He's not a baby anymore, but I can taste the fear even still.

He practices back-floats in the bath. He makes waves. He's in trouble if he sloshes too much water out of the tub. He dislikes washing his hair, which is copious and curly and a delight. When he was three and had a bad fever he slept on me for hours, waking only briefly to whisper that his "curls hurt."

It took me over a year to begin to write again after he was born. I was freaked. I couldn't relax. I didn't know how to let go. I didn't trust that it would come back, that I would come back. Insanely confusing time. I had a beautiful man and child. With them I felt anxious and trapped; apart from them I felt anxious and lonely and cast off. The problem, quite obviously, was me. I wrote my way out. I am ashamed of my faithlessness.

Starbucks

In the midst of horrid urban sprawl, on a four-lane road lined with car dealerships and half-abandoned strip malls, new gas stations, abandoned gas stations, parking lots, restaurants that serve nothing that qualifies as nourishment, here's this soothing global chain.

Nearby are the tiny Jewish guild cemeteries founded back when this would have been way out in the countryside. Albany Jewish Tailor's Assoc. Albany Jewish Stonemason Assoc. Now the cemeteries are crowded by malls and gas stations and motels and car dealerships and big box stores. If the weather's nice, take a stroll through a cemetery before settling down to work. Jewish law dictates that a child under a year old does not get ritually mourned. The children's section is rife with tiny headstones that say BABY OF MRS [whoever]. Or just BABY BOY.

When the kid was tiny and would only reliably nap in the car, this Starbucks drive-thru saved my bored, thirsty ass more times than I care to remember. I sat in this here parking lot for what must add up to whole days of my life. I amused myself by taking an ongoing series of car-nap selfies. Look here: I was still an artist. The car-nap-selfie series would surely change the way people thought of early motherhood and urban sprawl. Instagram much preferable to the infinite silence of writing. No dozens of orange heart notifications occasion completion of an insightful sentence.

Across the highway are the malls, oh please, not the malls, anything but the malls. Everyone looks like death warmed over, the walking dead. Zombies don't *know* they're unhappy, right? Or is it precisely the appeal of newfangled undead narratives that there might be zombies with angst? I thought the whole issue with zombies is that they lack the depth, the consciousness, the temerity, the bravery, the *decency* to wrestle with angst. To *understand* that they're unhappy.

Anyway, the first mall was built on a geological rarity: the Pine Bush. Habitat of the New Karner butterfly, so named by Nabokov. Valiant   protests   by   environmentalists notwithstanding. We call this first mall the Democrat mall, because it's showing its age and is so circa 1984 ugly it's almost sort of cute and everything about it is so shabby and second-rate you have to love it a little. (Excepting the pristine Apple store, which belongs in the second mall, really.)

The second mall is known as the Republican mall, because it's newer and shinier and there's a rambling Cheesecake Factory that might as well be a nineteenth century Opera House for the way the McMansion crowd gets dolled up to go wait in line there on weekends. Spanx city.

Both malls are depressing as shit, needless to say, unless it's the dead of winter and you just need to get out of the house, in which case: what a treat! The Democrat mall's not so bad around three or four on school days right when the kids are starting to gather, because suddenly there's this infusion of life instead of just the shuffling zombies, all of whom look about four decades older than they are, no one can stand up straight, lots can barely walk, they hobble, they limp, the women are losing their hair and people wear these permanent expressions of surprise and fear. Because movement and "nature" and fresh air and clean food and water and a quiet burial plot under some trees far, far from a highway are 21st century luxuries, marks of extraordinary privilege. Because lots of people have surrendered these things, or been robbed of them, or some nefarious combination therein. But you can buy a new outfit on the cheap at Old Navy, yay. During the first Iraq war, mall security infamously ejected a man wearing a "Peace on Earth" T-shirt.

But back to the Starbucks across the highway. They're playing old-old Billy Joel. There's a beautiful pre-op trans-femme barista. I'm cross-legged in an upholstered armchair in the back drinking an iced tea. A man just sat down in the next chair. We share a side-table. He's reading the Travel section. He's tapping his foot to the old-old Billy Joel. He looks lonely. He's got nice energy, a turquoise pinky ring. Possibly I'm projecting about the lonely part. Possibly I'm projecting about the nice energy part. We say nothing to each other.

The community bulletin board by the toilets is glaringly empty.

The train
Down to NYC and back home again the next day every few weeks. A vacation, a parallel life. I wouldn't beg Amtrak for a residency on one of these barreling overpriced old tin cans, but it's not so bad so long as no one left trash/food/perfume on your seat earlier in the route. So long as you have your headphones and a book and a tabloid and some snacks and your notebook and a pen and a seat on the river side and are dressed for the weather. Just so long as you don't forget your headphones.

On break at the food co-op
It was lonely, moving up here. I joined the co-op straight away. Figured I would find my people.

It was made clear that to be nominated for a slot at the cheese counter was quite the honor. All the cool people work in cheese. Produce might beg to differ, and bulk seems kind of fun, but in cheese there are free samples, and a boom box, and the beloved cheese monger, who is given to fits of operatic Italian.

The co-op's a mile from downtown, tucked behind a Family Dollar. Soon it will move to a hotly contested new building even further from downtown, but closer to the highway. There will be more parking, gleaming poured concrete, a bigger café, and shiny everything, but people will complain bitterly that it has lost its soul.

For now, soul intact, it's a charming rabbit warren with a tiny potholed parking lot and an appropriately surly, dread-locked staff. There is a beautiful personified sun painted on the wall by the produce ("Hi, sun!" my boy calls out in greeting) and a blue sky with fluffy clouds painted on the ceiling ("Hi, sky!").

My maternal great-grandparents owned and ran a grocery

store in Larksville, Pennsylvania. Met at an immigrant dance on the Lower East Side, got married in rental attire at sixteen, seventeen. Had four boys and four girls. The boys all died at or before birth, from "some genetic thing they can fix like *that* today," my mother tells me, snapping her fingers. RH factor, it's called.

Can you imagine? Four dead baby boys. Rabbi said no funerals for the dead boys, just showed up with a shovel and accompanied my great-grandfather on a walk in the woods to bury them. Seems harsh not to be able to ritually grieve a baby, but it was only practical: a few dead babies were par for the course. You'd be in mourning all the time if you went through the whole rigmarole every time. I think of my great-grandfather with the shovel, those tiny inanimate bundles, one after another. Where did he bury those boys? Was there a marker? Was he the kind of man who cried?

But the four girls all lived. And went to college! Louis and Dora Levinson, immigrant grocers too busy staying afloat to ritually mourn their four dead baby boys, sent four girls to college in the 1930s. Girls! To college!! During the depression! Can you imagine?

Great Aunt Miriam, the youngest of those girls, tells me the Polack kids used to chase her home from school, throwing rocks, shouting *dirty Jew, dirty Jew*. But it's also said that Dora and Lou were fairly popular in town despite being dirty Jews, since they extended a great deal of credit to many coal-mining families during the hardest years. My mother's cousin Lou, named for his grandfather, tells me all this. Latter-day Lou lives in the grandest old stone house in town. He's an obstetrician.

"You're so lucky," Lou says of my having given birth perfectly fine at home without scalpels or needles or electronic fetal heart monitoring or drugs or forceps or whatever other routine barbarism people are routinely brainwashed into believing they need. He also used to love to torment me about feminism when I was like nine. Lou's alright, though. His loyalty to Wilkes-Barre, to the family, to our common history, is admirable. He's the pride and joy of the whole immigrant narrative, and he knows it.

Dora lived to be an old, old lady, obsessed with American soap operas (from which, it's said, she eventually learned English). She lived to see her four daughters grow up and have children and she lived to see her grandchildren nowhere near the working class. She lived to be an old lady in plastic cat-eyeglasses on a chain, in a top-of-the-line recliner with a gorgeous brown and yellow and orange zigzag Afghan she made, watching soaps.

There's one picture of her and me. She's smiling, reaching up to squeeze my infant hand, but she doesn't hold me. My mother, her granddaughter, is blond and beautiful and educated and privileged and bananashit crazy, a world and a half away from whatever shtetl hut Dora's mother's mother kept clean. A world away from four dead baby boys buried without fanfare God knows where near Larksville, Pennsylvania.

Anyway, the key to grocery life is FIFO (first in, first out). I receive delivery from the organic dairy in Cohoes. The delivery guy has one of those interesting faces you can't stop seeing. In a yoga workshop, instructed to send loving kindness to someone we see often but don't know well, it was his face that came to me.

The co-op is good work. Better than teaching writing, possibly. The pay's probably not so different. I have room to think here. Mindless pricing, breaking down boxes. Lots to observe. An announcement over the muddy PA sounds like *David Grossman, line 1. Philip Roth, line 2.*

Terry is my shift-mate. We price and stack egg cartons. He tells me about his big Italian family, his cute boyfriend, the marathon he is training to run.

The assistant cheese monger is funny and fraternal and blushes outrageously over not much.

It's someone's job to guard the meat, to sit in a chair opposite the cheese counter and make sure no one steals meat. Word has it there was a spate of meat-stealing recently, so now someone sits, keeping watch. We bond, the meat watcher and I, when he tells me about his wife's impending homebirth.

Someone in produce offers to sell me weed, but I have a superior source already.

There's a guy who scares me. Easy to imagine him shooting the place up. People would say, "Yeah that guy, he always seemed a little off." People always says that after someone shoots someplace up. I avert my eyes, try not to be noticed. I will play dead in the event of a shoot-up. I will curl face down under the counter and play dead and he won't notice me and I'll live to hug my family and suffer constant nightmares forever after. Or maybe it will happen at the mall. One of the two malls. Which mall will it be? Or maybe it will happen at the school. Oh please, please, please not the school.

I am invited to select a CD for the boom box one day. I am thrilled. But it turns out the cheese monger can't stand Bob Dylan. *You just don't understand him,* I say. It is the very wrong thing to say.

I scribble in my notebook when there's something worth scribbling. *Are you writing about us in there,* they ask. *No,* I say. I invite them all to a party but no one comes.

I get frequent comments about what I'm wearing. This is one of my least favorite things about living here. Sorry if my outfit is calling attention to itself. It makes me happy. I miss New York City. Don't trouble yourself over my tiny opacity, to paraphrase Roth.

I start to feel like I'm in high school, where every conversation is sort of over my head but degrading in some way because I'm weird and my clothes are wrong or my clothes are right or I'm not cute enough or I'm too cute or who the fuck knows. And I'm supposed to laugh at myself. Or not laugh. It can be exhausting to live in a cosmopolitan place where everyone is oh-so-sophisticated and of the moment and worldly; that can be stifling and irritating, too. But I long for it sometimes. I'm not allowed to wear anything you don't recognize from the mall?

The scary guy seems to chill as the weeks roll on and I stop trying to smile or make eye contact, just lower my head and say "yes" or "got it" or "sure" or "no problem" when he tells me to do something. He seems to like me better, to relax a little, when I behave this way. So the eye contact was the problem. All my stark-naked smiling.

Madonna's in my headphones, singing "Gone": *I'm not... I'm not very smart.*

I run into my husband's ex. I'm like a foot taller than she is. Ungainly, forever fifteen—beastly, breasted, bearded—towering above the cute compact girly-girls. How could anyone want to be friends with me? So huge, bumbling, awkward. Also, it makes me nervous that she used to sleep with my husband *and* a former lover *and* not one but *two* favorite writers. (Not all at once, I don't think.) I don't care; I'll be Sister Wives if she wants. I'm fine with that if it means we share the work.

There's this other person I see regularly pushing her cart around. She is pretty and has a toddler and I think, in the annoying way I tend to think: "We are totally going to be friends!" But she is cold and does not respond to my dorky overtures and even though I'm sure she's just "shy" or some shit I of course wind up strangely hurt and cold in return. Which is exactly where being desperate for community gets me. Which is exactly why I have to stop this ridiculous "we are totally going to be friends!" crap. I get right up in her face one day, just for the sake of it, and say "Hi." It's like some form of punishment, my "hi." Like: I see you and I know you see me and pretending otherwise only adds to the unhappiness in this difficult world, so what exactly does it cost you to say hello?

I'm learning how to keep myself to myself, let people slowly earn my confidence. This might sound obvious to some, but I'm slow. (*I'm not... Not very smart.*) Thus far I have specialized in zero boundaries, almost like an ethos, and it has rather sucked.

I chose Dylan's "Most of the Time" when it was my turn with the boom box. *Turn that maudlin shit off,* the cheese monger hollered. Then he did the easy, mocking Dylan impression. I played it loud, later, while I did the dishes at home.

The months wore on and every Friday there seemed to be

some better thing I needed to be doing. Like writing. In my little office, or leaning against the doorjamb by the bath, or at the Starbucks out by the mall and the cemetery, or on the train. Because the novel was close to done. And I had this obvious realization: the sooner I stop spending Fridays at the co-op, the sooner I will finish my novel.

And writing! What a relief. Because writing is not about making friends.

(Guernica, 2013)

A HAPPY MOTHER, DAMMIT

THE SEDER LOOMS. Much to be done. Clean the house. No hunting crumbs with a candle and feather, but I do like a clean house. Maybe plant some bulbs, is it too late for that? Or too early? Clean up what the melting snow reveals: trash blown into the garden, last year's murdered houseplants. Get the guest room ready! Make a grocery list! So much to be done. One thing at a time.

The trick is not to make a perfect home. The trick is to make a *happy* home. Set the tone. A shared responsibility, to be sure, but you know what my mama used to say? "If mama ain't happy, ain't nobody happy." It's funny she used to say that, because she was so, so unhappy. (Mama, why? He would have done anything to make you happy. We all would have. You had everything.)

A small seder this year. Not like last year, the whole neighborhood crammed in around borrowed folding tables and chairs. Who doesn't love a seder, such rich and fascinating ritual? Springtime, renewal, the earth coming alive again. We are reborn, we are released. We'd hunt for eggs on Easter if we were Christians, but we happen to be Jews. We are the exception around here. A neighbor lady keeps inviting me to church, no matter how many times I say no thanks and remind her that we are Jews.

Anyway, it's spring: Pay attention! Feel the metaphorical implications in your bones. We didn't have this in southern California, seasons you feel in your bones. We had seder, though. We had two. We told the required story of redemption. We told it thoroughly. We turned to the correct page in the Haggadah, and we read aloud. We helped set and clear the table. I sang the four questions, year in, year out, proud/embarrassed youngest child. But it wasn't joyful. She was *ba'al teshuva*, meaning "returned" ("born again"), and she wanted to do everything to the letter. It was tense, stressful. Heavy. We weren't happy. What was the point of ritual? Why didn't some rabbi take her aside and say Hey, lady, cherish your family, chill out about the religious observance, just have *fun*, spirit of the law over letter of the law, look out for the health and happiness of your marriage and your kids, be happy, we'll all be dead soon enough! Where was that rabbi!? What even is the point of being a rabbi if you aren't helping people manage their bullshit?

My mother-in-law and brother-in-law are coming to help me cook. It's nice to be in the kitchen with people who like to cook. Some believe that the nourishing quality of food is determined by the energy of the people preparing it. There will be no banging furiously around my kitchen, muttering about how ungrateful everyone is. I'm making seder because I want to make seder. The people who like being in the kitchen can work in the kitchen. Those who don't like being in the kitchen can go run around in the park, throw rocks at what's left of the ice in the pond. They'll wash the dishes later, probably. Or they won't. I'm not keeping score.

Kids are exquisitely calibrated to their parents' emotional state. I am the mother now.

"Are you getting stressed out?" my little one asks when he hears me take an especially deep breath.

"Yes," I tell him, and exhale, and meet his eyes, and smile so we can both relax. We happen to be Jews, and so we inhabit the rituals of this holiday. But only to a degree, and only as ourselves, not at the expense of our joy, our peace, our selves. If the observance gets in our way, if the observance drains or hijacks us, if the observance browbeats or discounts us, if the observance becomes a burden we can hardly stand to bear, the observance can take a hike.

My house is a mess, but my children are happy, as a friend likes to say. The seder is a lot of work. Maybe I'll improvise at the last minute and forget the saltwater or parsley. Maybe I'll take a nap instead of dust. Maybe I'll meet the deadline of this essay instead of Xeroxing and stapling all my favorite bits from ten different Haggadahs.

Perfect hostess, perfect Jewess, running the show, force my kid to sing the four questions, hand-felt frogs for an original skit about the plagues, innovate some new way to make matzoh taste good, don my silk caftan like the high priestess badass postmodern homemaker *balabusta* bitch I was born to be, not a hair out of place, the table gleaming?

No. I demand my freedom. Here is my slave rebellion, an uprising worthy of telling: a happy mother, goddamn it. Reclining. Every fucking hair out of place.

(The Forward, 2015)

VAGINA JAIL

I GO SEE the new mothers as soon as possible. College friends. Cousins. Neighbors. Colleagues. Friends-of-friends. I make food, sit, fold laundry, do dishes, fetch groceries. I want them to feel seen, heard, human. They tell me how birth went down. I come to dread this part. The look in their eyes as they sigh or shrug or burst into tears or all of the above. Then they say *Whatever, my baby is here, my baby is alive, we're both alive, that's what matters, let's not talk about it anymore.*

Bullshit, I never dare say. *You matter too. What happened to you matters.*

So, I write a novel about a woman in the wake of birth gone awry, which I hope might exhaust my obsession with women in the wake of birth gone awry. It doesn't. So, I design and teach an MFA seminar about the literature of the childbearing body, which I hope might exhaust my obsession with cultural treatment of the childbearing body. It doesn't. So, I sign up to become a birth doula. Why not make it official? Give a name to what I've got, this fixation. Let people hire me, seek me out, pay me, value what I've learned, what I've seen, what I know.

It's an icy winter weekend, and we are eighteen women in a six-hundred-square-foot tenement apartment in Harlem. Let the consciousness raising begin! My fellow trainees are a nurse, a personal trainer, a college senior at work on her thesis, a dozen moms of small children, a Jehovah's Witness, and my friend R. We're all interested in reproductive health. Several gave birth via routine intervention, were treated questionably by caregivers, and got righteously furious. Several admit to being obsessed with birth. One refers to doula work as a "calling."

Our trainer is Leah, the Bronx's own Venus of Willendorf. She asks us to introduce ourselves and our maternal line as far back as we know. Reproductive females are born with all our eggs (unlike reproductive males, born with no eggs, who manufacture sperm on demand), so we actually somewhat existed within our maternal grandmothers and great-grand-mothers, Matryoshka dolls back to the start of time. I am Elisa, daughter of Elaine, granddaughter of Bea, great-granddaughter of Dora.

Dora had eight babies under the care of a midwife, four boys and four girls. All four boys were stillborn or died within hours. Bea had difficulty getting pregnant. I have no idea how she gave birth, but I'm familiar with American obstetric protocol from the 1940s: she was likely unconscious, tied to a bed, shaved, given a routine enema and episiotomy, acted upon with forceps. Elaine had three babies, three routine epidurals, episiotomies, and forceps deliveries. Her OB was very hand-some and refused to answer any of her questions. *You don't want to know,* he'd tell her flirtatiously. I gave birth at home. My careless, irresponsible homebirth midwife was MIA for all but the final twenty minutes of my thirteen-hour posterior labor, then neglected to do a postpartum visit. There are a lot of different ways for birth to go awry.

A good way to understand the role of a doula (Greek for "female servant") is as normalizer of pregnancy, birth, and life with a newborn. When we're ignorant about or freaked out by something, it cannot be considered normal.

"A good doula has a warm heart," Leah says by way of open-ing. Problem is, I'm short on patience since I took up the cause (or it took up me). I get sarcastic, I lose my cool, I bust up dinner parties, I roll my eyes, I lecture, I condescend. I know

I'm hindering my cause, but *Jesus*. How does one find equipoise in the midst of so many repetitive, heartbreaking stories? The patterns and themes so obvious, I want to scream. Birth violence seems like the last culturally sanctioned form of violence against women.

I'm here to put this unwieldy outrage, this corrosive anger, to good use. I want to link arms, take to the streets, storm the maternity wards, protect our sisters from fear and intimidation and protocol and routine and trauma and shame and loneliness and confusion. About one in ten women legitimately require medical intervention in childbirth. Trained pathologists are good to have on call. But please, let's be clear: We are not here to talk about that minority.

Leah has a beautiful grin. "In order to birth well," she says, "a woman must turn off her mind." We don't tend to question the efficacy of birth when we talk about mammals in general. Fundamentally, birth *works*. Our species would not exist if it didn't. We review the phases, progression, physiology, and psychology of healthy labor, none of which is esoteric if you're the least bit educated about birth; problem is, most of us aren't. The process has a rhythm and cadence all its own. It can go on safely for quite a while. The cervix softens and opens. If she has scar tissue (from overzealous pap-smears, HPV treatment, abortion, previous C-section) it can take longer. If she is immobilized and/or temporarily paralyzed, it can take longer. If she is anxious or fearful, it can take longer. If she is in unfamiliar surroundings, it can take longer. If she does not feel "safe," it can take longer. Once the cervix is fully open, the urge to push. Delivery of baby, delivery of placenta, restitution. An efficient and complex progression, never exactly the same, tied inextricably to any given woman's feelings about her body, sexuality, history, family, self (see also: the mind).

(*Fuck that*, I hear so many people say. *I needed intervention, I would have died without intervention, I loved my epidural, I loved my doctor, my baby would have died without...* Okay. Okay. Okay. Then this is not about you. Go find yourself reflected absolutely everywhere else.)

A vast wealth of evidence points to physiological benefit of sympathetic women close at hand in relaxed, familiar surroundings. Laurel Thatcher Ulrich's Pulitzer prize-winning examination of the diaries of 18th century New England midwife Martha Ballard is an invaluable resource in establishing a safe, efficient, healthy history of birth. French physician Michel Odent has been beating this drum for decades. British doula Rebecca Schiller's *All That Matters* has lately picked up the cudgel. Physiological birth requires encouragement, stamina, and calm, continuous support. It's helpful if the lights are low. A relaxed body can open. The fearful mind is noise. Beyond thought, a primal wisdom exists. I'm so freaking bored by pseudo-intellectuals who insist on denying the mysticism of the body.

(*Fuck you, don't make me feel bad, I wanted all that woo-woo shit but my baby was going to die and I was going to die and...* Okay. Okay. Okay. That sounds really hard, and I'm sorry; we're not talking about you.)

Oh, the brain, what to do about the stupid brain, forged by Hollywood, by every birth scene ever faked for film, by vague inherited trauma, by horrific pileups of It-Happened-To-Me? The brain can muck everything up. The brain believes birth is a narrowly averted tragedy with haunting Kate Bush soundtrack (remember the 1988 rom com *She's Having A Baby*?). The brain believes Meryl Streep in *Heartburn*, wherein she's frantically rushed to the hospital in early labor, frantic, shrieking, gasping, terrified. Soon she's on her back, oxygen mask over her face. Guy in a lab coat reads a machine printout: "There's something wrong! We need to operate now!" When she wakes, her husband is smiling at their baby and the terror is depicted as having zero fallout, all that gasping and shrieking and threat and major surgery of no consequence whatsoever. The brain believes an episode of HBO's *Girls* in which a wacky character, *herself* purportedly a doula, attempts a critically premature unassisted home birth and is carried, protesting, down the street to the hospital, where she is surgically delivered of a child who goes immediately to the NICU. Then two main characters break up whilst holding hands over the incubator.

Then the mother is shown serenely happy, arms empty, hopped up on drugs.

We examine the extremely common (but rarely medically necessary) practice of artificial labor induction. I raise my hand. All research (to say nothing of common sense) supports a hearty no to routine or elective induction. The drug widely used is synthesized from cattle pituitary and causes contractions that are 10 to 100 times more powerful than normal, with no reprieve between contractions. It all but requires anesthesia, which can slow progress and interfere with pushing. It often puts the baby in distress. One formerly-popular labor-augmenting pharmaceutical, a peptic ulcer medication used off-label, led to one too many ruptured uteri led to one too many dead women and babies led to one too many lawsuits, so now it's fallen (mostly) out of fashion.

But we're here to become doulas, not to bemoan reality. Be practical, my fellow trainees tell me. If a woman is giving birth under obstetric care, she is likely to be routinely induced. She is likely to be given a spinal. She is likely to be immobilized. She is not likely to question. This is the way things are. We're here to become doulas. We must work within the system.

"No," I say. "I don't want to work within the system. The system is suspect. We all know the system to be suspect. Why be complicit by working within it?"

"Look," Leah concedes. "The first intervention is leaving your house. The next intervention is putting on a hospital gown." With her first child, a daughter, she had commonplace complications caused by routine intervention. She says what everyone says: "I didn't know any better. I did what they told me." She's quick to clarify: "I am not here to talk smack about obstetrics." She goes on to say, however, that after doula service at a hundred births over five years in hospitals all over Manhattan, Brooklyn, Queens, and the Bronx, she no longer attends planned hospital births: "I saw enough," she says quietly. I aspire to be more like her: reasonable, level, kind, steady. She is exactly who you want as your doula. She knows what's up, but she's not full of rage. Anger just corrodes the vessel. Anyway, who wants a corroded doula? A warm heart is where it's at.

Mainstream birth culture makes me want to light myself on fire in protest, is the thing. That's what brought me here, to this cramped room on the fourth floor of a tenement building in Harlem. Outrage can be problematic and off-putting, but it's also the seed of action. What productive activism isn't fueled in part by rage?

Watch the woman, not the clock: this is the mantra of decent labor support. Watch the woman, not the calendar. Watch the woman, not the monitor. Watch the woman, not the machine. Birth generally responds well to trust. As, come to think of it, do children.

We review hospital regulations, which make hospital staff sound like police. Triage, anonymous nurses, hospital gowns, recycled frigid air, nothing to eat or drink, timed labor. How to outwit them? How to sneak some crackers or juice or soup, get out of bed and move around, hide all the healthy, normal impulses of a body in labor? For a healthy woman to have a decent birth in this kind of setting would seem to call for a combination of intrigue and luck. "Don't get on the nurses' bad side," Leah advises. "Make friends with the nurses."

Two trainees realize they had the same OB at the same Manhattan hospital, and giggle about how she's known for marching into the room literally swinging her forceps.

"Oh, and what about Dr. T," laughs another. "He comes in and stands there while you're pushing and goes 'Don't make me cut you.'"

"That's not funny," I snap. Here we are trading tips about how to navigate the flagrant abuses and threats of modern maternity wards, how to evade stressful protocol, how to shield the laboring woman so she can progress efficiently in peace and quiet.

"I would have liked to give birth at home but my husband wasn't okay with it," a trainee says. Here is yet another bummer trope: the spouse who dictates where and how the woman births. Others nod, like that's to be expected. They're pragmatic, my fellow future doulas. "Look," they say. "Women are afraid of childbirth. Everyone's afraid of childbirth. Fear of childbirth is in our water, in our air, in our genes. What can you do?"

I dunno. Maybe, like, revolt?

Think of *Children of Men*, set in a war-torn world where babies are no longer born. When a destitute young woman gives birth to the first baby in almost twenty years, the infant's cry silences the fighting, halts time. Soldiers put down their guns and fall to their knees weeping. What is more important than new life? Who is more important than the person who labors to bring it forth? How dare we fail her? How dare we be silent or complacent about the ways in which we ourselves were failed?

Day two, R and I oversleep. We take the train to Harlem and climb four flights of stairs to the little room.

"Back to vagina jail," I mutter.

R laughs: "Are you disappointed in the level of discourse?"

Indeed, I am disappointed in the level of discourse. Consciousness isn't seeming too freaking raised.

R smiles, older and wiser: "It's just how people are."

We watch a childbirth education film from the 1950s. Pack a suitcase... drones a male voice, while a woman with a blank face carefully does so. Bring makeup... to make you pretty. The blank woman is escorted to the hospital, where the husband waves her off and takes a seat in the waiting room. Everything is sterile. The camera pans over gleaming metal tools and machines. In the next shot, birth is presumably over and done: a nurse wheels an occupied bassinet into a nursery. What happened? What is not shown, and why? Are we too delicate or dumb to handle our own realities? Are we not to be trusted with our own bodies?

"When I arrive at the hospital, I want a glass of whiskey, I want the epidural in my back, and I want to be hit in the face with a baseball bat. And just wake me up when it's over, because I've seen the videos, and it looks terrifying," actress Kristen Bell told *Us Weekly* in 2013.

This apartment is not a suitable space for a group our size. I feel caged, crave movement. In another video, elder doula Penny Simkin helps a woman find her rhythm. Rhythm is key. Labor is dance. Labor is effort. Labor is active.

We examine a study in which respect and affection in labor equals higher postpartum self-esteem. Leah phrases it more poetically: How will she remember this?

I've lost count of the privileged, pedigreed people I know with awful birth stories. Women with Ivy League degrees, names on book covers and office doors. Women who can build bookshelves, support themselves, make meringue, helm companies, toss around academic jargon, sew a dress. When I say awful I mean she doesn't understand what happened or why. Awful meaning someone else was in charge. Awful meaning she will not discuss it ever again. Awful meaning she wishes she could do it over. Awful meaning she was prescribed psychiatric medication afterwards because she couldn't stop thinking about it, couldn't sleep at night, couldn't relax with her baby. Awful meaning she wonders if it had to be that way.

Anthropologist Robbie Davis-Floyd, in her monumental *Birth as American Rite of Passage*, offers this: a woman will find comfort in the rituals of her belief system. If she has been raised to fear birth, to see her body as dangerous and the doctor as safety, then the rituals of medical birth (machines, bright lights, air conditioning, restrictions, invasive tests, lack of privacy, steel instruments, narcotics, gowns, needles, numbness, surgery) will be reassuring. You cannot tell a woman who has been raised this way to simply chill, go home, put on some music, trust her body. (Well, you can try, but before too long you'll find you're just glowering over the desert course like a witch on trial.)

"Maybe you should be a midwife," someone tells me on a break. "You're so, like, passionate."

I hoped doula training would be a haven for my indignation. I assumed we'd rail against the system and brainstorm ways to subvert it together. I was hoping for a roomful of renegades, fellow furious radicals. A place to be unabashed.

We watch a woman in Mexico giving birth in her adobe, surrounded by her family. There is pan flute accompaniment. In early labor they go for a walk down to a stream. When they return, she's ravenous, eats a huge lunch. A while later, labor gets intense, and she dances around the house with her husband and their two boys, moving unselfconsciously. Finally, after some hours of good, hard, celebratory work, it's time to climb into the big, tiled bath, where she delivers her little girl. The newly minted big brothers immediately climb into the bath to hug and kiss and marvel. Everyone is laughing and crying, whole and healthy and intact and well. (Cue lame jokes about the cleanliness of the bathwater.)

Now it's time to talk business. Most doulas don't claim income on their taxes. I find this hilarious. So we're not willing to subvert the man in the medical industry, but we're cool subverting the man in government?

"I'm not saying anything about it," Leah says.

The personal trainer shares a long story about clients trying to bargain with her, concluding with the observation that if a client tries to "Jew you down," they're going to be a nightmare.

What the fuck? No one else seems to have registered any offense.

We segue into a discussion about the word "advocate," which one woman says makes her "uncomfortable" because it sounds too much like "adversary."

"So, like, if you say you're someone's advocate it implies an adversarial relationship," she says.

Wrong. The latin prefix *ad-* means *toward*. To ad-*vocate* is to help someone toward a voice of her own. To be an ad-*versary* is to move toward conflict.

"It's your job to support the woman in whatever she wants," the nurse snaps at me.

Oh? In her ignorance? In her terror? No. That is not my job. And I will not do it.

"The labor room isn't the place for politics," Leah says.

"Well, *obviously*. But everywhere else sure as shit is." Like right here, in goddamn *doula training*, in Harlem, at the start of a new century, as mind-boggling numbers of women and babies in the United States are being violated, then sent home and told to be fucking grateful. I mean: human and civil rights for women are all in vogue now, right? We've come a long way. Arguably the most beloved entertainer of my childhood got roasted alive on the spit of our collective disgust and will die in prison because turned out he's a serial goddamn rapist. We seem finally to have arrived at some understanding that women's bodies are... our own? So it seems like now would be a *real* good time to question what's going on with birth. Now would be a good time, while we're at it, to talk about how women of color in the U.S. have hugely disproportionate maternal and neonatal mortality rates. Yesterday would have been better, but now's okay. Tomorrow's too late.

Birth Is Not a Feminist Issue, declared the headline of a garbage Elle Magazine opinion piece in 2015.

The undergrad, who thus far hasn't spoken a single word, chimes in: "I'm not a feminist or anything, but..."

"Are you fucking kidding me," R says.

All hell breaks loose, and Leah excuses us for lunch.

My doula told me to imagine I was standing on the shore with waves crashing over me. *Duck under the wave*, she advised. *Go into it.* I held on to her for dear life. *Don't let it crash right into you*, she said, *see it coming and dive right under it*. The power of her words! I clung to them, to her. I needed very badly to hold on to someone, and there she was, with me all the way. *Under the wave*, I repeated senselessly. *Under the wave. Under the wave.*

I don't want to do this, I said. *I don't want to do this. I can't do this. I understand why people don't want to do this. I can't do this. Please don't make me do this.*

You are *doing it*, she repeated. *You're doing it. This is it. You're doing it. This is it. You're doing it.* And in that way, I did do it. I was doing it. I did it. It was difficult and scary and absolutely fine, and I did it. It was the hardest thing I'd ever done, and I did it. Where would I have been without my doula? If I'd had the standing offer of a sweet spinal, a "just in case" surgical team all scrubbed up, tapping their feet impatiently, the vague threat of my baby dying, a sea of furrowed-browed strangers,

my partner freaking out... I am a hundred and twelve percent
certain I would not have been "able" to do it.

Some third cousin once removed invariably wants to know:
Weren't you scared something would go wrong? Look: it was a
healthy pregnancy and I had good prenatal care. Had complications arisen, I would have been referred to a pathologist.
Something can always go wrong, hate to break it to you. That's
the excruciatingly hard part: we are mortal beings. There is no
escaping the possibility that things can go wrong. Sometimes,
yes, women and babies used to die in childbirth. Then we
started washing our hands before sticking them into body cavi-
ties, which has saved more lives than every other medical
advance combined. And women and babies still occasionally
die in childbirth. Life, death, what can I tell you? We don't
always get to say.

Finally, on the third and final day of training, we get around
to discussing useful tools for attending labor. Negative
thoughts and words are dangerous. The laboring woman is
psychic. Fear and excitement are hormonally identical. Keep
your voice low, breathe with her so she remembers how.
Model calm. Be her mirror. Give her a rhythm. Follow her
rhythm. Follow her lead. Be consistent. Be quiet. Be solid. The
laboring woman is not polite. Don't take anything personally.
Take off your shoes. Show respect for cultural differences.
Make eye contact. Go with the flow. Anticipate her needs.
Movements should all be downward. The left ear is somehow
better for whispered encouragement and sweet talk. Remind
her to keep her jaw loose, her noises low and deep. Beauty
secret: grab a little of the baby's vernix, it's the best moisturizer
on earth. Why would you wash a baby immediately after it's
born!? "They don't come out your ass," as Ina May likes to say.
The logistics of being on call.

Jew-Down keeps using the word "transcend" when she
means "descend."

And what about the role of the husbands/partners?

"I have two kids and a husband, so... three kids," someone
says.

"It's normal to hate your husband," says another.

"During labor my husband was totally inadequate... as usual," says a third.

For once I'm circumspect. My husband was the bomb in labor. Bully for me. Though I did hate him for a while postpartum.

Now a C-section video. The patient has severe fibroids. Hallelujah for the reliable tool of surgical birth in such cases. Incision through eight layers of skin and muscle tissue, into the uterus itself, cauterizing blood vessels along the way. A burning smell. Takes twenty minutes, much longer than I imagined. *You'll see here, the doctor's made the incision a little on the small side, so there's some considerable tugging to get the baby out.* Five minutes of yanking and pushing and pulling and two pairs of hands and is that even a living body? Two living bodies? Finally: a baby. They replace the woman's internal organs and begin to sew up the eight layers of muscle tissue. Atrocious procedure. For this woman it was crucial. Not so for the majority who undergo it.

I had a C-section and it was no big deal and I love my baby and all is well and I'm great with it so fuck off, it doesn't matter, people often scream in public, but I have never, not once, heard anything remotely like that in private. It's fashionable to obscure the issue as a matter of personal preference rather than a systemic issue with disastrous public health consequences, which is a sophisticated tool of silence, because to press the issue is ultimately, oh dear, *impolite.* Zero working familiarity with the physiology of normal childbirth is both an unfortunate prerequisite *and* consequence of this dynamic. Last summer my seven-year-old niece proudly informed me that babies are born when the doctor decides it's time to cut open the mother's stomach.

Most birth workers I know are of a mellow sort. They simply don't engage where they're not wanted. Some confess to having shut down a dinner party or two in her day, but seriously, why bother?

But I have to wonder: When people refuse to engage with a particular issue, what the hell is going on with that particular issue?

In Susan Sontag's notebooks there is the briefest mention of her son's birth. She writes only that it was "difficult," and that she "wanted not to know anything." She was nineteen years old. She was put under. Imagine: Sontag, one of the most voracious intellects of the century, *wanting not to know.*

When training's over, Leah gives us each a starfish and an allegory about a boy on a vast, starfish-strewn beach. He spends all his time walking up and down the shore, tossing starfish back into the ocean so they won't dry up and die.

What are you doing, asks a nearby old man. *You'll never be able to get all these starfish back into the sea. You can't make a difference to them all. Yeah,* says the boy, picking up another and throwing it. *But I made a difference to that one.*

I chicken-out on talking to Jew-Down before leaving, but later I send her an email, as calm and understated as I can manage, about how "Jew down" is not a decent expression and I hope she'll reconsider using it in the future.

She writes back immediately: she would *never* use such a terrible expression! I must have misheard her! The expression she used was *actually* "chew down." I don't bother to explain that there is in fact no such expression. This woman has been hearing that phrase her entire life, and she has absolutely no clue what the hell it is she's parroting. How profoundly apropos! I say I'm so glad I misheard her, and wish her the best.

Certification requires documented attendance at three births, along with a mountain of paperwork and some administrative fees. Women find me via word of mouth, one after another. I attend three, four, five, six births. All transcendent (and descendant, for that matter) VBACs, two at home, though I ignore the paperwork each time, unsure what I'm after with this enterprise. Personal fulfillment? Career change? An essay?

It's wild, what begins to happen when I identify myself as a doula: women of all stripes light up and lean close to confide about miscarriages and birth and fertility and contraception and cycles and abortions and breastfeeding and sorrow and struggle and triumph and defeat. I'm privy to a world of ecstasy and pain and death and hope and fear. And sure enough, my old outrage dissipates. I have all the work I can handle. Way more than I can handle. There is no energy left for outrage.

How could I have confused *talking* about it with *doing* it? Man, is there a lot to do. Text a woman who was due last week about how hard it is to wait. Bring food to a woman with a newborn. Fold laundry for a woman with a toddler and an infant and the flu. Make a woman in early labor giggle. Hold a woman's hand in the middle of the night, walk laps around the L&D unit, keep on keeping on. Gather resources for a woman who wants to get off hormonal birth control. Text a woman in her fourth month, remind her it's okay to take it easy. Pretty endless. Best I can figure, this is what it means to be human: Band together at the beginning of life, band together at the end of life. And maybe periodically in the middle as well, but we're all busy and you can't force people. Some, you can feel their resistance at a hundred paces. Best to give them a wide berth.

"I have to decide whether or not I want a C-section," a pregnant person volunteers at a party. My husband cracks up and backs away.

"That's a big decision," I say cheerfully. "What are your thoughts?"

And then, when it's clear she doesn't have much interest in thinking about it at all, I say: "Hey, have you tried this hummus? It's super delicious!"

"I don't want them to cut my taint and I don't want them to cut me open and I don't want to poop in front of strangers," another young pregnant person confesses one bright fall morning.

I nod very, very slowly: "So... maybe you want to think about giving birth in an environment where all those things are less likely to happen?"

She shrugs: "I really like my doctor."

My son is into The Wizard of Oz lately, and I am startled by the first question Glinda asks Dorothy: *Are you a good witch or a bad witch?* How interesting: the implication that she must be one or the other. The implication, as I take it, that we're *all* one or the other.

THE SNARLING GIRL   75

I'm not a witch at all, Dorothy demurs, and Glinda looks puzzled.

We are different after we give birth, different than before, and too often not for the better. Did I take up the cause or did it take up me? Elisa, daughter of Elaine, daughter of Bea, daughter of Dora, daughter of I don't know, daughter of I don't know, daughter of I don't know.

(The Cut, 2016)

WINTER, ALBANY

.

HER NAME WAS SALLY. Sally-bo-bally. The Salster. Sometimes we called her Butt-Wiggle, for the way she shook it when we came home. Butt-Wig, for short. You know how it is with nicknames, the language of love. We found her photo on a rescue organization's website. Sally! She was bright-eyed and smiling. Hi! Someone had tied a jaunty bandana around her neck. I adored her on sight.

She was up for adoption the following Saturday in a parking lot behind a warehouse in Schenectady. I'd never had a dog. My mother said it was dirty to have animals in the house.

We resolved to keep open minds and meet all the dogs on adoption day, let the right one find us, not force anything, but it was always going to be Sal. She stood on her hind legs and wagged her whole ass at us. She was practically dancing. Sally-Sal! Jet black, with a short, shiny coat. Pit/lab mix? Pit/lab/hound? Pit/whippet/lab? Who knew. Who cared. The chemistry was perfect. Love at first lick. Not like poor little Buddy, over in the corner with a bad case of worms, or pretty retriever Julius, who wouldn't look anyone in the eye. It was always going to be Sal. Four months old, spayed and vaccinated. No one else showed the slightest interest in her. She was ours. We filled out the paperwork and took her home.

Her eyes! The way she looked at you and didn't look

away. So present and soulful, a real lover. She was like a *person*, if we're talking about the most honest loving open deep good authentic funny sort of person, and how many of *those* have you ever met? She'd curl up next to you, close as she could get. She wasn't happy unless she had her body in the sweetest, closest possible proximity to yours. She was like one of those rare massage therapists whose touch feels psychic: exactly where you want it, exactly how you want it. Magic.

I was never into dog memoirs or whatever, never understood that mad devotion to pets. Seemed weird to be that into an animal. It seemed, to be honest, fairly *sad* to be that into an animal. Like, why don't you find yourself some more *people* to love? I didn't get it. Now I got it. People are way, way overrated.

Sal was our sweet darling beloved lil' boo. I was done having babies. How creepy I find it when people talk of "completing" their families, as though a family is a construction project or a vocational course, a finite thing, a theoretical ideal. How moronic and shortsighted and hubristic I find that attitude. It's like the ugliest kind of nationalism, on a microcosmic scale. And yet. And yet. Sally gave us three something new to love, and in so doing gave our family a new dimension, this whole new love to share between us. I felt a weird, delicious sense of... completeness. We were in love with her and in love with each other and in love with the way she loved us back and generally high off our own abundance of love and good fortune. There was this warmth in my chest. We re-drew our goofy family crest to include her. We sang ridiculous songs to and with and about her. We spoke to her in a silly dialect. Dare I say it? We were happy.

A new puppy (like a new baby) is a full-time job. This part I had not anticipated. Life got very narrow for a while. You have to keep them from eating things that might kill them, clean up their puke and shit and piss all over your home, and make sure they play and rest in equal measure, so they don't lose their minds. I didn't have the heart to crate-train her, just as years earlier I hadn't had the heart to sleep-train the baby. Her favorite toy was a rubber ball done up to look like the head of the Statue of Liberty.

The dog park became our haunt. We made lots of new friends. Never quite up to snuff on the human companion names, but the dogs were indelible. Odie, Cinnamon, Abel, Sidney. When the weather was still nice you could sit on a bench and read or veg out on your phone while they frolicked. The hour before sunset there were often twenty, thirty dogs running in packs. Lucy, Luna, Paddy, Poppyseed, Gigi. With the humans you might discuss the weather, or the origins and social dynamics and ages and temperaments and breeds and habits of the dogs. Once in a great while you might discuss what you did for work, where you lived relative to the park, or how you felt about local politics. Never national or global politics, however, noooooo. You didn't have to discuss anything with the dogs. You just had to keep your knees loose while you stood around, lest they come up running behind you and knock you over. One time, I saw an old lady go down in such a way, which wasn't funny. And a young lady, another time, in the snow, which *was* funny. As it got colder and colder still and even colder and then even *colder* and colder than *that*, only the die-hards remained. Moose. Gunther. Yogi. Harper. The human small talk became ever more distilled. We wore coats over our coats and stood around meditating on hot chocolate and interspecies love.

Early on, Sally was rolling and wrestling joyfully with a little fluffy brown dog when the brown dog's mistress stomped over: "If you don't get your dog away from my dog, I am going to fucking kick the shit out of it."

I was speechless. There must have been forty dogs running around, happily wrestling. "This is a dog park," I said. "They're playing. They're dogs. This is how dogs play. If you have a problem, you shouldn't be here."

"Get your fucking dog away from my dog," the woman hollered. A small boy stood by her side, staring at the ground.

"These are dogs," I said again, very slowly. "This is a dog park." The small boy sneaked an incredulous glance at me. He was clearly not used to anyone standing up to his mom.

"Get the fuck away from me," the woman yelled.

"I'm sorry, buddy," I said to the little boy. "You deserve better."

"Don't fucking talk to him," the lady screamed. But then she backed away.

"Sometimes there are crazies at the dog park," someone shrugged after she left. I never saw that lady again, but I think of that little boy whenever I hear the Neko Case song "Nearly Midnight, Honolulu."

Sal was a shitty leash-walker. You'd get welts on your hands trying to keep her in heel. One time I made the mistake of trying to carry a fresh latte-to-go while walking her, and of course I wound up wearing that latte. "You fucking cunt," I hissed at her, dripping latte.

Off-leash at the park she was okay but inconsistent. She was obsessed with squirrels. Occasionally she'd run off, go on a little joy ride. This was a little scary and a huge pain in the ass. We'd run after her, swearing and sweating. Once she ran off an hour before a friend's wedding, at which we were all set to perform honorary duties, and we narrowly avoided missing the ceremony altogether.

Our rad local dog trainer recommended the documentary *Buck*, which is about horse training. But the principles of animal communication are the same: fellowship and energy exchange in action. We watched *Buck* four times. We got *way* into *Buck*. On a deeper level it's about how to deal with anger. How to discipline and communicate fairly, humanely, decently, and intelligently. How to be honest with oneself about the destructive tendencies one carries from one's forebears. It's about parenthood, really. It's about every kind of relationship, really. It's about the soul, really. You gotta watch *Buck*.

There are a few traffic roads in the park, and the dog area, though enormous, isn't fenced, and local drivers are notorious for ignoring the speed limit and pedestrian right of way and being totally assaholic in general (much like… drivers every-where), so we invested in a training collar (which is a euphemism for shock collar). But Sal's joyrides were infre-quent, and we were in and out of the park three, four, five times a day. Usually if there were other dogs around to play with, she wouldn't dream of running off. And usually if we had treats she was responsive, obedient. So it seemed silly to go through the whole rigmarole of the "training collar" every time. Sally was a good girl. Sally was a great girl! It felt awful to strap her into that collar. She plainly despised it. Anyway, what kind of person wants to shock a dog into obedience? We were reluctant. This is called foreshadowing.

After Thanksgiving, the park is transformed by an annual display of elaborate Christmas lights. The Police Athletic League puts them up, with sponsors such as Key Bank and the *Times-Union*. Everyone loves or hates or loves and hates those lights. They charge cars $25 admission to drive though the park after dark. Lines of cars snake around throughout November and December. People can't be expected to *walk* through a park looking at Christmas lights, now can they? This is America.

In her first snow, Sally leapt and bounded, astounded and ecstatic. The calendar year wound down and a new one took its place. January was a hangover of ice. I had a hard bleed with the by-now-expected accompanying hormonal migraine. And then there was the problem of the dentist. Namely, that I needed to go to one. I'd been putting it off for ages. A bunch of old fillings were breaking down, there was some new decay, blah blah etc. I kept putting it off because I wasn't in pain, and because I was busy. Also I have a bit of a trust problem with doctors. But I kept hearing my father's voice: *Don't make the same mistake I did.* He'd ignored his teeth for years and wound up completely screwed, to use a technical dental term.

So, New Year's resolution was to go to the dentist, be a grownup, take care of my teeth. Did you know that dental health is closely linked to general health? I read up. Our mouths, these obsessive gateways, are harbingers of disease. I asked the oracle of the neighborhood Facebook group for recs, and liked the look of a guy right over on Dove Street. I liked the idea of not having to get in my godforsaken car to go to the dentist. Very Mayberry.

He was a kindly, soft-spoken gentleman from Kew Gardens

with a degree from NYU Dental. His wife was his receptionist. There was classical music playing in the dinky little office. Okie-dokie. First order of business: replacing an old filling on a molar. Dr. Soft-Spoken said we should do a crown, because it was a rather large filling to begin with. I was pleased with myself for "being a grownup." I was pleased to live in a neighborhood with a kindly soft-spoken dentist just around the corner. He removed the old filling, drilled the shit out of the tooth, took measurements for a permanent crown, and fitted a temporary. The epinephrine in the novocaine made me nauseous. He promised to make a note of that and use a different brand next time. I was to return in two weeks. The temporary crown hurt, but I was assured it would subside. I trudged home in knee-high snow and took Advil. Sal curled up with me on the bed and licked my face and tucked her head gently into the place between my shoulder and jaw.

I had booked myself a New Year week in an Airbnb in my favorite woodsy town an hour away. Beats application fees for writers' residencies, plus simple travel and access to home/family, plus no other writers sizing me up over dinner. I smooched my family and loaded up the car. My hosts were a mom, dad, and two kids whose shrieks provided the soundtrack to my lonesome days and nights in the private studio attached to the back of their house. On my last day, the mom was apologetic about the noise, but I assured her I didn't mind.

"Do you have kids?" she wanted to know.

"I do," I said, smiling the beatific smile of a woman who has spent her reproductive years *doing it all*.

"How many?"

"Three," I lied. I even believed myself, for a second there. Three kids! However did I *manage* ? Oh, you know, you do the best you can. It's like a backpack full of diamonds: heavy but precious. I felt like a religious icon for a second, there. A biblical matriarch. The real deal.

"Wow," she said, slightly lowering her head in deference to my higher station. The more children a woman has, the more of a woman she is, after all. Then she got a look I've seen on women with no children, one child, two children, three children, four children: *Have I Done Enough?* "I would love to have a third," she said, "but I..." She shrugged and rolled her eyes and sighed. "Maybe in a few more years."

"It's a lot," I said vaguely, from my faux-lofty maternal station.

My heart raced. I did not have three children. Why had I lied to the nice mother-of-two? What the hell was the matter with me? This was a small town; we probably knew people in common.

My own mother had three children. Three beautiful gifted healthy children, a ridiculous bounty. But it didn't make her happy or proud. Quite the contrary. The last time we spoke, months and months ago, she informed me that no matter what I ever accomplish in life or love or work I will always be a failure.

How often have I been made to feel terrible about "only" having had one child? How often have I been forced to listen to lectures about how "sad" only children are, how a family isn't *really* a family until there are multiple children underfoot, how #siblings are #whateverthefuck, how the more kids a family contains the happier a family it is, how a family isn't *really* a family unless it looks like a Norman Rockwell painting? Oh, do you *just* have one? Oh, do you *only* have one? You must be a cold, selfish woman to deny your child a sibling, huh? You must have really loathed childbearing to fail to reenact it, huh? What's the matter, don't like being a mother? Don't love your kid? Why else would you *only have one?* Don't you find chil- drearing to be worthy of your time and energy? Guess not, if you *just have one.*

Just! Only! Just! Only! I fucking get it, okay? I get it. My family, no matter how loving and solid and decent and strong, is *not enough.* I am not a full/true/real mother. I'm a dilettante mother, a sort-of mother, a half-assed mother. I am not as mother as all you other mothers, I get it, children are trophies, the woman with the most is the champ, any fewer than the standard basic two is a perversion of nature, a blow striking at the heart of everything sacred in society and culture and life itself. I get it I get it I fucking *get* it, okay?

I'd experimented with spontaneous lies before. A few years back some dumbo was holding forth about my duty to "give" my son a sibling, and something in me snapped. "Oh, I couldn't agree more," I said with puppy-dog eyes. "It's just that all my other babies died."

Twas a wild pleasure to watch her face crumple in on itself, and an even greater pleasure to be avoided by her thereafter.

Or how about the jocular elbow to the side from the woman who proudly despises childrearing and mistakes me for her comrade: One and DONE, amirite?

No.

I took a long walk in the woods as the light faded to a deep blue, and then it was time, mercifully, for bed. Sex is cool, but have you ever called it a day when the sun sets in the late afternoon in the dead of winter? I ate some soup, watched a stunning Mike White movie about a flawed dad taking his son on a college tour, and slept until the sun came up again.

Sal went bananas when I returned home. She shook and grunted and leapt and twirled and tried to high five my face with her face. My human family members were pleased to see me, too.

The day came for the permanent crown. The temporary had never felt right, and I'd been living on baby food, but I was being such a wonderfully stoic grownup about it, have I mentioned? I tiptoed carefully down Chestnut Street on sheets of ice. After Dr. Soft-spoken numbed me up with the epinephrine novocaine ("Oops," he whispered, "forgot."), he yanked the temporary off with some plier-like apparatus and fumbled around to fit the permanent. After about twenty minutes of messing around, he apologized: it didn't fit. The lab had made a mistake and would have to redo it. He would re-measure, put on a second temporary crown, and I'd return in another two weeks.

I continued to play the role of stoic grownup. This was life. Things could always be worse. Soon enough it would be behind me. It was like wintertime in New England: you had to live it out, survive it, trust that it would pass. I tiptoed carefully back home on sheets of ice up Jay Street, mainlined Tylenol, and showed my son Steve Martin as the sadistic dentist in *Little Shop of Horrors*. Sally never left my side. I had the obvious dream about all my teeth falling out.

Two weeks later, same scene at Dr. Fuckup's, only this time, after the pliers and twenty minutes of fumbling with the permanent and the apologies and the suggestion that the lab redo it again and I return in *another* two weeks, I freaked out, got out of the chair, demanded my money back, and called a fancy dentist in Saratoga, begging him to see me right now, today.

"I'm very sorry," Dr. Fuckup kept saying, softly. "I am very sorry."

The fancy Saratoga dentist *re*-measured for a permanent, put on a *third* temp, and told me, judging from the x-rays, that a crown hadn't even been necessary in the first place. Oh! And that the root of the tooth might be so traumatized by all this excitement that we'd best keep our eye on it for a root canal.

Could things get worse? I woke up the following morning with my head, neck and shoulders frozen in excruciating pain. Impossible to move, talk, sit up, lie down, breathe, be awake, or be asleep. Was very sorry for myself. Canceled my day and made every kind of wellness appointment. Acupuncture helped a little. To the massage therapist I said: "Please handle me like I'm an injured premature newborn."

In between my efforts at recovery Sal lay with her head on my belly, or with a protective paw on my shoulder. I could do nothing but stare out the window at the barren trees and occasionally shuffle off to seek treatment. Physical therapy was twenty minutes away by car. I had to get Sal out for a walk before I left. She did her business on the sidewalk, and I headed back toward the house, but she went on strike. *Nope,* she said, *I'm gonna sit down right here and you're gonna take me to the park, over thatta way. Have you forgotten the park? We need to go to the park.* She was insistent, the stubborn little bitch. *C'mon,* she said. *Please!?*

I couldn't resist. She was so smart and funny and good. "Fine," I told her. "Five minutes." We'd already been to the park for an hour in the morning. She had frolicked with Cinnamon.

We were going to go back at sunset, like we did every day. This dog did not want for park time. But fine, fine. Five minutes. The sun was out and the sky was a perfect sky blue. When had the sun last been out?

It was a Friday. The dog park was empty except for us. Late January. The sun felt so, so good. Do you know where this is going? Of course you do.

They were removing the elaborate Police Athletic League Christmas lights. There was a truck. White, unmarked.

There was a squirrel across the pedestrian road. Sal went for it. Grinning, I swear, with her ears flattened back against her head and her tongue flapping in the wind. She was in her glory, running for that squirrel. The truck was barreling up the pedestrian road. *Pedestrian* road, have I mentioned? The truck neither slowed nor stopped. I saw her running, and I saw the truck pass. I was just over the crest of a small hill. My heart stopped, but I thought: she probably made it to the other side. She was fast as hell. But then I didn't see her on the other side. Why wasn't she on the other side? I knew. My breath knew, caught in my chest. Then I crested the hill and saw her: a heap in the road. The truck sailed right on out of the park.

A young man in a bright red down jacket was sauntering up the (*pedestrian!*) road. I was holding on to a low branch of a tree, screaming a horrible shallow impotent high-pitched unfamiliar scream.

Is she dead? Oh my god, is she dead? Is she dead oh my god is she dead is she dead? The young man in the red jacket approached. I couldn't move. I thought maybe she was still alive and I should go to her, touch her, talk to her, hold her, *tell* her something. Tell her I loved her, and…what? That it would be okay? But I couldn't move. My screams were terrifically shrill. Hideous sounds. I didn't recognize my own voice. This was a cliché I had heard before, and here I was, embodying it, shrieking my fucking head off. I should *go* to her, *hold* her, tell her it was okay, tell her I loved her. Maybe she was still a little bit alive. Maybe she could still receive a bit of comfort and love. Why couldn't I move!? *Sally.*

I just held on to that tree, keening, despairing of my

inability to move, and despising myself. Was I afraid to get *blood* on my clothes? Is *that* how totally fucked up and stunted and useless a creature I am!? What if she was still even the tiniest bit alive? What if she was even the *teeniest* tiniest bit alive, and I didn't *go* to her, touch her, hold her, talk to her? "Sally oh my god Sally oh my god Sally." It wasn't even my voice. Whose voice was it? Some pathetic lady whose beloved puppy was lying dead in the road while a big heedless truck full of Christmas lights disappeared up Henry Johnson toward the interstate. Such stupid repetitive shit, I screamed. Is she dead oh my god is she dead oh my god is she dead oh my god oh my god oh my god oh my god oh my god oh my god is she dead is she dead is she dead. I screamed until my throat closed up, and then I screamed some more.

The young man in the red jacket bent down to look at her. He was calm. It wasn't his dog. Perhaps he had grown up on a farm, where animals die all the time. He nodded: Yes, she was dead. I couldn't get anywhere near her and I couldn't stop screaming. Sally. The screams came from someplace I'd never been before. Sudden violence, deep and irrevocable cruelty, mortality asserting itself unexpectedly. Shock. Grief. Bam. Dead. Sal.

I was one of those people, not long ago, who didn't see what the big deal was when a pet died. I mean: it wasn't a *person*, right? I mean: sorry your cat / dog / bird / bunny died, but I mean, yeah, that's *life*, right? Anyway, why don't you go get yourself some more *people* to love!?

A young man in all black with lots of piercings and a big rucksack came walking by. And, from another direction, a woman with big green eyes, on her lunch break. These two were suddenly next to me on the grass by the tree. I wept and wept. They held me and spoke to me. The guy in the red jacket hung back.

"Look at me," said the young man all in black. "She will always be with you. She's with you, she is in you, you have her in your heart forever no matter what, there is no death." It was something. I took it. The young woman told us *her* beloved dog had just recently died and she was still "not over it." I held on to these strangers and wept some more. I cried my baby, my baby.

I know she was just a dog. Only a dog. Just. Only. Just. I know.

My husband Ed came running with an old wool blanket. We wrapped her up and carried her back to the house and laid her in the garden under the wind chime. It was time to pick up our son from school. We went in together, holding hands, our faces raw. "What's wrong," he said, the moment he saw us. Back at home we knelt and put our hands on her and had a good cry. Then we took her to the vet and left her there to be cremated. They gave us a room to be in with her for as long as we needed. I'll be praying for you, said a kind woman at the reception desk.

I texted the strangers in the park: I don't know how to thank you guys.

I slept with her Statue of Liberty ball. It smelled like her. I held it to my face and sobbed myself to sleep, hoping she would show up in my dreams. What else can the dead do for us but that small, merciful favor? I woke from dreams in which she did not appear and I sobbed some more. We all huddled in bed together. I couldn't bring myself to empty her water bowl. I considered drinking what water was left. I didn't change out of jammies for a week. I watched *Fun Mom Dinner* twice.

I kept seeing it happen, kept reliving it, kept replaying the whole day, tormenting myself. Why had I acquiesced to the dog park? I didn't have *time* for the fucking dog park. We had already *been* to the dog park. We would go again *later* to the goddamn dog park.

We drew a huge tribute with chalk at the spot where she died, and returned daily to refresh it, left discount old roses from the flower shop. It was cold, but for hours I'd sit there, relishing the cold, wanting to suffer, at the spot where she died.

Inexplicably, we went back to the rescue place almost immediately. "Sally would want us to go rescue one of her friends," our son insisted.

"Let's just go look," my husband said. "Let's just go see who's there."

"Whatever," I said. "Fine. We'll go get another puppy." Who cares. Let's get two. Four. Six. Eight.

There were a bunch of dogs up for adoption that day. They were all just dogs. There was no Sally. When Ed picked up a sweet 10-week-old shepherd hound mutt who'd avoided a kill shelter in Tennessee, I took her in my arms and felt nothing. She was scared and sad looking. Her name was Cara.

"Whatever you guys want," I shrugged. A woman from the rescue organization helped us fill out the paperwork. When we told her we'd already adopted a dog from this organization once before, she made a nasty comment about our suitability, as though we'd killed Sally ourselves, with our bare hands, for sport. Still, they let us take Cara home. For weeks I kept accidentally calling her "Sally." She was just a dog. I took care of her, but I could not promise to love her.

Was it a mistake, getting Cara so soon? She wasn't Sally. I desperately missed Sally. But it was nice to be busy again with a new puppy, and anyway, who can say what's too soon, what's right or wrong? Grief is an island. Was I trying to avoid grief? No, I felt the grief pretty freaking hard. Should I have continued to focus exclusively on grief? Doesn't life force enough of that?

A woman who'd had a stillbirth told me about how, the day they buried her baby, she asked her midwife when she could get pregnant again. She could think only of getting pregnant again as soon as possible. The midwife gently reminded her that she would never be able to get this baby back. She might have another someday, but this baby, the one she had wanted and grown and loved, this baby would not be coming back, and getting pregnant again would not change that fact. The woman refused to participate in this discussion. The woman told me how angry this discussion made her. Just tell me how soon I can get pregnant again, she insisted.

At the park with Cara I faced a steady stream of *Where's Sally?*

I relayed the sad tale over and over and over again. Everyone was duly appalled. *Was I going to call the City? Had I*

*called the police? Who was responsible for that truck!? It could easily
have been someone's child!*

I knew it wouldn't behoove me to go seeking justice from
some civic official or bureaucrat. It wouldn't bring her back. I
wanted to simply bludgeon all those even tangentially responsible, a la John Wick. After a couple weeks, however, I did place
an elaborately casual call to the Police Athletic League. I
requested Sgt. Whoeverthehell, who wasn't available. I left a
polite message with a secretary.

"May I ask what this is regarding?" she asked.

"Oh, the Holiday Lights," I replied airily.

No return call, so a few weeks later I called again, and left
another polite message. This time Sgt. Whoeverthehell called
me back. I put on my best fake authoritative/objective jour-
nalist voice and asked questions about the Christmas lights
cleanup process.

"I'm wondering who specifically was driving the truck on
January 26th of this year."

There was a pause.

"Is this about the dog?"

"Why, yes. Yes, it is about the dog. The dog. Indeed, yes. The
dog. So you are aware of the dog."

"Yeah," he said, "that was a terrible thing, the driver was all
the way up in Amsterdam by the time we got in touch with
him, and he said he had no idea he'd run over a dog. He's a
huge dog lover, got four of 'em himself, so he was very upset
when he heard."

"How odd," I said, "that he wouldn't then reach out in any
way to the young family whose dog he'd murdered. Being such
a dog lover and all. You do realize he was driving on the pedestrian road, too fast to even realize he had run over a dog? You
do realize we're talking about a park where human beings of all
ages and shapes and sizes come to walk around and play and
be. You do realize that it could easily have been a child."

Sgt. Whoeverthehell grew increasingly quiet and inarticu-
late. "Yeah," he said. "Yeah, that's too bad that happened."

"Yeah," I said, mocking his tone. "Yeah, it *is* too bad that
happened."

What was the point of this conversation? Nothing was going to bring Sally back. I let that useless shmuck get off the phone.

Spring was a long time coming. Late April, we were still wearing our heaviest winter coats. What a beautiful February night this would be, we joked on a frigid walk to hear Salman Rushdie speak at Page Hall.

I was away from home, sleeping in a big bed all by myself, when Sal finally came to visit. It was just before dawn. I was halfway conscious when I was suddenly filled with her absolute presence. Felt her with me, next to me, alongside me, her body right there, the way she used to burrow under the covers and press herself against my belly so I could feel her heartbeat. So intense. Here she was. Finally. Next to me. With me. Sal. Just saying her name brings me pain, which is one way of explaining how much I loved her. Sally. Girlfriend. Bestie Girl. Beauty Girl. Butt-Wiggle. Butt-wigs. Pee-Pee Paws.

You should have seen her running after that squirrel. She died happy.

I ran into the Airbnb lady at the cute bi-annual craft market at the lake house soon thereafter. I was with my son. There she was, manning a stall from which she sold whimsical hand-printed baby and children's clothing. She greeted me warmly.

"Is this your eldest?" she asked.

"Yes," I said. (And my middle, and my youngest!)

I hustled out of there. My funny boy looked at me quizzically, awaiting an explanation.

"I did something really strange and stupid," I told him. "Have you ever told a weird, pointless lie?"

Sorry I lied to you, lady. Sometimes it's necessary to slip into a parallel reality, that's all. I wanted to feel like a woman with three children for a minute. I was curious about what it might feel like to inhabit that life. I didn't mean any harm. I guess I wanted my mother's precise opportunities and blessings, only I wanted the chance to play out said opportunities and blessings differently. That's all. Just an odd attempt to try and change the narrative, right a cosmic wrong. Just the simple task of transforming the past/present/future for a brief, shining moment, you know? Only that. Just that.

I saw the red jacket guy around the neighborhood and in the park often. I waved the first time, but he didn't acknowledge me. I thought it was a fluke, but no acknowledgment the second or third time either, so I stopped waving.

I strap the new dog into that training collar every single time we go to the park, without fail. And *of course* I've grown to love her. The heart's a muscle.

(Longreads, 2018)

FIVE RECENT ENCOUNTERS, OR "ONE OF THOSE PEOPLE"

1. Yoga Teacher, December 2017

We met in 2011 when I happened into her small studio in the mountains. I liked her immediately. Great teachers are hard to come by. And sometimes even pretty good ones have their egos way out in front of them, which renders them essentially useless at best. But she was a great, great teacher: slow, calm, grounded, humble, soft, strong, exquisitely knowledgeable. After class she asked if I'd like to chat for a minute. It was a hard time; I was spiritually sunk. We sat together. She looked into my eyes. I broke down, told her all the things I was carrying. She didn't flinch.

I spent years studying with her, even invested in her studio. We traveled to Central America. She saw me through grief and trauma. I quite literally held her in my arms while she gave birth to her son.

After she became a mother she sort of let teaching go; handed over the reins of the studio to another teacher, Rick. He was very intense, masculine, and competitive. He had a way of making you feel like you had to push yourself farther than you really wanted to go. I was always borderline injured after a class with Rick. This made me angry with myself, angry with Rick, angry with yoga, angry with the patriarchy. I always swore I wouldn't let it happen again, but I let it happen again and again. Something about how he approached you on your mat, the way he would get a little too close, adjust a little too much, stare a little too hard, kind of dare you... I wasn't going to let him *win*, you know? Invariably I held his gaze, did as he said, and hated myself later.

Post-Rick-class one morning I went to my real teacher's house to hang out. We lay around giggling with the baby. I could already feel some upset in my neck and shoulders and hamstrings. I bitched about Rick's aggressive teaching, and about my own complicity and helplessness. We had discussed this many times before.

"Yeah," she said, "I don't know why he has to be so, like... aggressive... and intense... and... like... *Jewy*."

I closed my eyes, took a breath, let it out.

Really? Really?? Really!?

When I opened my eyes she wore an embarrassed smile.

"Shit," she said. "Did I just make a mistake?"

I looked at her sadly. My friend. My teacher. Mi hermana.

"What the fuck," I said.

"Look," she said. "I just... before I moved here I was just never around these kinds of... intense... New York... people."

I chose sadness over anger. I became the teacher. I sat there looking at her. I told her in an exceedingly calm tone that she might want to examine the roots of that kind of thinking, find out what exactly she was carrying, where she got it, and ask herself if she really wanted to continue carrying it, if she really wanted to pass it on.

Her sweet baby giggled as he pulled himself up to stand.

"I'm sorry," she said. "Are we okay?"

"We're okay," I told her.

It wasn't true.

2. Neighbor, February 2018

Her father is Jewish; her mother is gentile. She wasn't raised Jewish but now puts a menorah alongside her Christmas tree on Instagram. She is on her way to becoming a nurse, getting prerequisites done at community college. She has to take all these challenging science courses. She gets along really well with her lab partner. She sends a group text to a bunch of us, her friends: *You guys, I'm in love with my lab partner! The other day he goes 'oh, you're Jewish? No wonder you're so smart!'*

I write back *pls tell your lab partner that ethnic stereotypes are never cool even when they happen to be complimentary.*

(I neglect to add: …even though many of us are guilty of promoting these very stereotypes ourselves so that we can feel superior and somehow powerful in the face of so much historical and ever-present bigotry and oppression and the fact of being so pitifully outnumbered in the world at large! This is so boring and obvious! There are smart Jews and dumb Jews and rich Jews and poor Jews and tall Jews and short Jews and pretty Jews and ugly Jews and fat Jews and thin Jews! Please get a fucking clue!)

She sends an embarrassed emoji, and we do not speak of it again.

3. Lyle Lovett, March 2018

He and Shawn Colvin are in concert at the Troy Savings Bank Music Hall. Class acts, both of them. Lyle especially: what an amazing performer and songwriter. We're big fans. Seen him three times in the past five years.

The show is a sort of storytelling night, the two in chairs onstage with their guitars, trading songs and stories. Very cool, very chill, very much an audience full of elderly white people. Lyle gets to talking about his Lutheran upbringing: "Martin Luther, now there was a complicated feller! He wasn't the greatest guy, but a lot of good came from his work. Like Hitler and the Autobahn!"

The audience half laughs, half groans. Lyle turns scarlet, but that famous grin of his is wide as can be. The show goes on. Later, he asks Shawn about her tattoos. She tells him some stories about her tattoos and asks him if he has any.

He goes: "No… no tattoos… I always wanted to be buried in a Jewish cemetery… A Jewish cemetery in a cozy corner near the Autobahn."

4. Montessori Teacher, April 2018

A progressive, excellent, self-satisfied private school in the boonies. Are we the only Jewish family here? As in: raised Jewish, educated Jewish, married Jewish, keep kosher, remember the Sabbath and keep it holy, plus a bunch of other esoteric shit I don't want to get into just now? Seems maybe we are.

A teacher with a thick southern accent once told me her maternal grandmother was Jewish "but didn't want anyone to know it, so she would never admit to it."

"So that means *you're* technically Jewish," I told her.

She laughed a polite southern laugh and said, "Oh *no*, honey! I don't *think* so!"

"See you on the trains," I muttered whenever I saw her.

It's a lovely school; I don't want to be sour about it. Officially it's very inclusive and whatnot. Overwhelmingly white and suburban, though hard not to notice how the promotional materials and billboards often heavily feature the like nine black/brown/Asian kids. One (white) mom runs a book club featuring exclusively Black literature.

They're always nice about welcoming me to come in and talk about Jewish holidays. Who doesn't love ethnic snacks? I bring apples and honey for Rosh Hashanah, doughnuts and dreidels for Hanukkah, matzoh and plague puppets for Pesach.

One spring morning I go observe the fourth-grade classes to see which classroom we might prefer next year.

A teacher is doing a lesson on the rug in the corner with six or seven kids. He's written *World Religions* on a white board. *Hinduism*, he writes. *Islam. Buddhism. Christianity. Animism.*

(Animism!? Animism.)

"What else," he asks.

"Judaism," one girl offers.

The teacher writes *Other*.

"There are a lot of other religions," he says. Then he writes percentages next to each group and instructs the kids to use the info to draw a graph, because the lesson is ostensibly about learning to draw graphs.

5. Neighbor #2, April 2018

Ran into her crossing the street and stopped to chat. She's just back from a trip halfway around the world. I'm just done hosting a ton of people for seder.

She says: "You're really into all the Jewish stuff, aren't you."

I say: "Well… we're Jewish."

She says: "But you're more like one of those *cultural* Jews, like it's not your whole *identity* or anything.

I say nothing.

She goes on: "I mean, you don't like wear a *wig* or anything."

I say nothing.

She goes on: "There were some of *those* people on my flight, and *those* people are so *interesting* aren't they?" She says this with a face like she just got dog shit smeared on her shoe. "I mean, like, you're not like one of *those people*."

"Actually," I say, "I am a lot like those people."

(Lilith, 2018)

DIVINE SPARK

ON THE RADICAL FEMINISM OF
PHILIP ROTH

READING Philip Roth has always felt like a private affair. Not *secret*, as my mother says, but *private*. From my first encounter (can't tell you which book it was; my memory's shot), I loved Roth and I loved his work, and in those days it would have offended me to make any distinction whatsoever between the two. Any writer worth reading—male, female, tall, short, fat, thin, white, black, brown, Jew, rich, poor—bleeds on the page. I knew this instinctively long before the MFA, thankfully, so the MFA couldn't wrench it from me (not for lack of trying). Any writer worth reading opens a vein and generously shares the flow.

So cutting my teeth on Roth meant that my bullshit meter was set, early on, to high. If I set Roth's baseline honesty, his willingness to, as they say, "go there," against others' writing, I found most others' sorely lacking. Which, yeah, made me a tough creative writing workshop participant and then, later, teacher. Cutting my teeth on Roth made me a rather extraordinary bitch. Or maybe that's not fair; probably I was always an extraordinary bitch and cutting my teeth on Roth just freed me to develop my bitchiness alongside—or maybe even in lieu of—"craft," such as it is. Any writer worth reading calls upon endless reserves of self-awareness, self-flagellation, and a healthy sense of the absurd. Any writer worth reading spares *no one* due critique: not characters, not readers, and most especially not God, aka the writer herself.

To put it more simply: the guy gave me permission. Still does.

But I have to confess that a lot has changed for me as a reader and writer and human over the past few decades, and I haven't stayed as singularly faithful to my beloved Roth as I might have sworn I would. He's still sacrosanct, still the gold standard, still how I identify my own work within the constellation of contemporary literature. But I got sort of... sidetracked. I got into some other stuff. Childbearing. Therapy. Marriage. Middle age. Gardening. Instagram.

Also, as you may be aware, a lot has changed in our culture. You may have heard about the seismic shifts afoot: it is no longer considered cool for men to behave like oversexed pigs, to objectify and use and discard women. I mean, it was never really *cool*, but now it is *mainstream* uncool. We live in interesting times.

I don't read much *about* Roth, anymore, either. The raft of obituaries, in particular, I avoided like the plague, particularly those written by fellow writers, each of which came off like an all-too-pervasive social media humble-brag: I got coffee with Roth! I wandered the Natural History Museum with Roth! Roth once gave me advice! We shared an unforgettable sandwich! He invited me to swim in his pool! I can boast none of those distinctions. Indeed, for a long time it was a source of some angst that he had never responded in any way to my old, moderately infamous meta-fictional fan letter, which, it must be said, I personally placed in his hands after an intensely charming talk he gave at Columbia University around 2007. Which is maybe why, over the years, I drifted away from my single-minded adoration of the man and his work, the work and its man. Unrequited love gets boring eventually, even for a masochistic obsessive like myself.

He praised Nicole Krauss, he "mentored" Lisa Halliday, he was chummy with Zadie Smith; what the fuck, dude? Why not *me*? What was wrong with *me*? Too tall? Too broad? Too intense? Too Jew-y? Too loudmouthed? Too desperate? Too bloody? An uncomfortable reflection. His bastard daughter. Or maybe, worst of all, *not a good enough writer*. Brutal. Okay. Whatever the case, I wasn't granted entry into the club. My bumbling efforts at establishing real-time/space connection with the great man proved fruitless. So I went on my merry way. Go where it's warm: probably the single best piece of writing advice I ever got, and pretty useful with regard to relationships in general, too. All I can tell you is that those obits pissed me off. Each felt like the unmistakable *thunk* of dirt performatively dumped onto the coffin by an all-too-eager mourner. But I'm not here to talk smack about Nathan Englander.

At a Jewish burial it's considered a great mitzvah to actually shovel dirt into the grave. Three times with the shovel handle upside down, because we are distinguishing between the act of planting something that might grow, something that might bring us new life, and burying the dead, who are dead. Then again, three more times, with the shovel right side up, to signify that regardless, new life is always just around the corner again, we hope. It's these mystical aspects of Jewish ritual that make Judaism worthwhile for me. I'm susceptible to the mystical shit.

It's considered a great mitzvah to do the work of physically burying the dead because the dead cannot repay it. But if you've ever been to a Jewish burial, you may have noticed how it goes after members of the immediate family—the stars, the VIPs—have done their dirt-dumping. A line forms. People get into it. Something about physical labor and grief and fear and uncertainty and self-consciousness and duty. My turn! Gimme that shovel! Me next! Ooh, me, me, me! A bit of a burying frenzy, inevitably. By the time it's over, the somber mood has changed, and everyone's ready to eat.

During the public mourning of Roth, I felt like old Mickey Sabbath in *Sabbath's Theater*, skirting the edges of his secret long-term lover's funeral, lurking. Who but the reader (God?) could ever know what they meant to each other, how perverse and profound their private relationship?

I skipped the symbolic shiva (read: wasn't invited), seized

the moment to sell the long-suffering first serial rights to that old, moderately infamous meta-fictional fan letter, cashed the check, and tried to get back to work. Ah, work: I've been chipping away at a new novel for almost five years now. *Endeavors in art require great patience*, as Roth once said, or wrote, or maybe it was his alter ego in the wonderful Halliday novel. The point stands.

But then came the invitation to speak to you all here today, and I wondered what would happen if I were to re-read *Sabbath*, the Roth novel I invariably name as my all-time favorite, in spite of not having read it in ages and truthfully not recalling many of the specifics. The fearlessness, though! That I recalled in my bowels. The base, unacceptable, hideous, real, fucked up, unafraid, beautiful openness of that book. Unapologetic to its core. Nothing whatsoever to lose. The embodiment of why novels matter, why art matters, and why moralism-in-art can eat every dick in hell. (Nothing against dick-eating.) (That's the kind of joke Sabbath might make, and yes, I know it's a bit on the provocative side for an academic talk, but the spirit of the subject must be thusly honored, and anyway, surprise! *I'm not an academic.*)

A symphonic portrayal of human frailty and filth: that was pretty much all I could recall about *Sabbath*. When I read it twenty-three, the writing blazed off the page, left me slack-jawed, riveted, amazed, appalled, in stitches. The things you could do in fiction! The grotesque and radical honesty you could get away with, if you could tell a decent story! It was definitely time to reread that fucker.

Concurrently, as it happened, I was teaching a feminist literature seminar at a legendarily progressive undergraduate bastion of privilege. *Impersonating* an academic, with questionable results. And so, over the course of the spring, as I slowly re-read and savored *Sabbath*, I was also prepping for my seminar, rereading Mary Wollstonecraft, Adrienne Rich, Audre Lorde, Mary Daly, Charlotte Perkins Gilman, Barbara Ehrenreich, Lucille Clifton, Harriet Jacobs, Florence Nightingale, Mary Shelley, Emma Goldman, bell hooks, Toni Morrison, and Grace Paley. And wondering, with increasing bemusement,

whether I might in fact be *the only person in the world* to not only
have read both Mary Daly and Philip Roth multiple times
throughout the years, but to stand proudly, insistently, vocifer-
ously, delightedly behind pretty much every goddamned word
of both. *Am I* in fact the only person in this vast, dark, mysterious universe who believes passionately in the righteous
furious nonlinear ecstasy of Mary Daly's *Gyn/Ecology* AND in
the foul spiraling sadistic poetics of the walking boner that is
Mickey Sabbath!? Correct me if I'm wrong, but I'm afraid I
might be, and it's a hell of a lonely distinction.

At casual glance, what is the *matter* with me that I'm not
bothered by Mickey Sabbath's libidinous nihilism? What's
wrong with me that his rhapsodies about his extensive
international experience with whores don't raise my feminist
dander one little bit? *How* am I not the least bit judgmental of
his sexual relationship with his college student? *Did* he murder
his first wife? Why don't I *care*?

Because Roth is a masterful, wily, incisive, and perfectly
deranged storyteller, of course. Because I'm having so much
fun. Because Sabbath is fully human *and* fully nonexistent.
Because it's fiction, which is the only place we are allowed to
be truly free. In reading (and writing) fiction, we get to suspend
for a blessed moment the need to be *right*. To be righteous, to
uphold what is right. To "behave" ourselves, to speak appropriately, to avoid offense, to toe the line. Fiction is, always was,
and ever will be the only place we never have to *lie*. Bad fiction
doesn't know this.

Anyway, it would be extremely easy to overlook the
simpatico spirit at work in Daly's Metaethics of Radical Feminism and Roth's Hymn to an Aged Boner on the Loose.

If patriarchy is indeed, as Daly so astutely posits, actually a
"religion of necrophilia," in which our planet earth and the life-
giving bodies of "women" are to be systematically destroyed,
co-opted, or caged to feed the greed and ego and power and
death-worship of "men," why then, poor old ruined, grief-
wracked, impoverished, helpless, careless, voracious Mickey
Sabbath—his beloved older brother Morty shot down in a war
machine at the end of WW2, his appetite for (consensual!) plea-

sures of the flesh unquenchable, his artistic genius sabotaged by... well, this is complex: by censorship? By diseased hands? By his own refusal to play nice? Regardless! Mickey Sabbath can only be on the side of the radical feminists.

To wit: He's non-linear! ("Trying to talk sensibly and reasonably about his life seemed even more false to him than the tears—every word, every syllable, another moth nibbling a hole in the truth.") He's anti-authoritarian! ("Behind the answer there is another answer, and an answer behind that answer, and on and on.") He's non-rational! ("In my experience the direction of life is toward incoherence.") He's disrespectful of cultural norms! ("To affront and affront and affront till there was no one on earth un-affronted.") Sabbath is an official emotional Hag, in the deepest Daly sense, tied immutably to his feelings, his grief, his rage. ("The mind is the perpetual motion machine. You're not ever free of anything. Your mind's in the hands of *everything.*")

He also refuses to let go of grievances. ("I'm fifteen, remembering this stuff. Emotions, when they're revved up, don't change, they're the same, fresh and raw. Everything passes? *Nothing* passes.") Finally, he's blasphemous! ("Despite all my troubles, I continue to know what matters in life: profound hatred.")

Sex is how Sabbath asserts himself against death. We all have our different ways of doing so, don't we? If we're lucky, we do. Unless the patriarchy's got us so numbed up on pills or mass media or sugar or drink or all of the above that we can't even barely begin to recall *wanting* to give death the finger. You have to feel to feel, you know? And oh, the glorious sweep of Sabbath's feelings. Oh, the offensive, gluttonous, hurtful, obtuse, obsessive sweep of this one little human being's feelings. (Hurt people hurt people.)

Remember what it was like to have an inner life? To enjoy fluency with thoughts and feelings and memories not dictated to you by the Twitterverse, not reflected back at you by advertising campaigns embedded within mass entertainment? To think thoughts and feel feelings not fit for constant sharing and validation? The glorious poetics of any given human bacteria meat ship's private idiotic prejudices, scars, traumas, greed, unfairness, and pure, distilled, desperate *need*?

Here is a man who is trying to live. He is sixty-four years old and says he'd like to die, says he intends to die, but there's a divine spark propelling him toward light, toward action, toward revolt, toward being alive. He doesn't, in the end, want to die. We'll all be dead soon enough, of course, yes, all of us, soon enough, but while Mickey Sabbath is here, he's not going to turn away from a single godforsaken opportunity to assert his here-ness.

On the question of Roth and women, women and Roth: I can't be bothered to care, and I don't *have* to be bothered to care, because I was never invited to swim in his pool, see? All I have are the books, which means he's no less alive for me than he was ten years back, or than he will be ten years hence. And for that, I thank him. Swimming in his pool would have overly complicated things. All I have are his books, and his books don't bear the slightest trace of bigotry. I don't have to wrestle with the flaws of the man himself, because the man himself is unknown and therefore irrelevant to me. His *characters* might offend, might delight in offense, might embody every kind of intellectual, emotional, psychic dysfunction, but Roth's so much smarter than that. You have to be a simple-minded jackass to fall for anything so straightforward as bigotry of any flavor, and Roth is no simple-minded jackass. Roth's interested, always, in the complexities of human behavior and emotion, in what drives people to behave like shitheads, to bust up their lives, to die alone, to deny themselves anything so nice and wholesome as healing and closure or any other sort of mystical hippie shit I personally happen to like. (Maybe *that's* why I never interested him as a writer: deep down, I'm a complete sap. Sorry, old man: one cannot choose one's offspring, try as one might.)

I feel crusty and ancient and confused and outraged and disgusted and impatient a lot these days, having maybe a little to do with the teaching gig at the notoriously progressive bastion of liberal artistic privilege. The world has *changed*. It's no longer considered interesting for a twenty-something creative aspirant to stand (symbolically or literally) before a great and powerful male artist and beg him to (literally or symbolically) impregnate her. It's no longer considered *cute*. Germaine Greer has been disowned by t-shirt feminists for insisting that cutting off one's dick does not make one a woman. Also the oceans are dying and the bacteria and fungi are outsmarting drugs, yes, and there's micro-plastic in everything and sperm counts are plummeting faster than you can say "unregulated fertility industry." Human nature and behavior and absurdity and hypocrisy and hubris and impropriety, however, remain much the same, as Roth reminds us it always has and always will. Great artists *reflect* the ugliness and unfairness in the world; they do not freaking *invent* it.

Of course I didn't fully appreciate, at twenty-five, what it meant to play off my youth and fertility the way I did in asking Philip Roth to pretty please impregnate me. At forty, I understand better, but I still love that story, which was composed in a feverish state, in one sitting, at a café on Wilshire Blvd in West Los Angeles called, I kid you not, *Literati*.

Rereading Sabbath has given me back what I'm going to be bold and sappy enough to call *joy* in the act of writing my own current monster/novel. It's given me back some of the excitement I've admittedly lost, trying to fit writing time in around domestic life, around small talk with Montessori moms, small talk with folks at the dog park, small talk of all stripes. Trying to fit writing in around impersonating an academic well enough to try and stand tall before the undergraduate liberal artistes. Trying to fit writing around teaching second graders at Hebrew School this year, a gig I needed like a hole in the head, but which I took because, let's face it, it's ridiculously great material for a short story. (Think "The Conversion of the Jews" as narrated by a perimenopausal witch with some serious personal failings and a real fucking dearth of patience, fiction being, again, the only place in which we never have to lie.)

I was young and confused, running on pure adrenaline, when I meta-fictionally asked Roth to impregnate me. It was a lazy request. Don't make *me* do all this hard work. I'll just lie here and passively *incubate*, for a fantastic round of applause.

This writing business is *tough*. Let my body do the work, give my mind a break, how about it? Maybe ignoring me was the most seriously the guy could take me: No such luck, girlie. Get your ass back to work.

Of course I want my new novel to be great. Of course I do. Or, failing that, I want it to suck super interestingly. I want it to fail rivetingly. Like Mickey Sabbath himself. Like everything flawed and shortsighted and slighted and wronged in the bizarre human race. And after that I want to produce a bucket load more stories, and another novel, some more weird essays and more novels, and I don't know, but I'm pretty sure this is what I'm here for. Creative fertility was always where it's at.

I never want to lose what I learned from Roth, is my point. What I learned to harness in myself from *reading* Roth: willingness to "go there," willingness to be obscene, to be flagrant, to be risky, to be unkind, to be brutal, to be *wrong*. Willingness to implicate myself, to stubbornly interrogate the weak spots. Because in the realm of fiction, it's all in the spirit of play. That's what makes it useful. That's what makes it valuable. That's what makes it possible. It's a way of practicing our fluency with the whole scope of human folly, so that when we have to look at the news, when we have to see the goings on in our feeds, when we have to deal with real-life characters, when we fuck up or we are confronted with the fuckups of others, we are never really surprised or shocked or confused or shaken. We already know how things are, and why. We know how *we* are, and why, even if we can't change a thing. This is how fiction makes us wise.

It wasn't until I had already invested a significant amount of time and energy into composing these thoughts for you that I realized what I *should* have done is simply write the guy a new letter. Dear Philip, round two. Check in with the old bastard, tell him what I've been up to. If we wanted to get *real* current, it could be a screed about the wild world of assisted reproductive technology. I could call in some Mary Shelley, propose we exhume Roth's body, extract some DNA, toil in a lab for a few years, and bring forth a flesh-and-bone heir to the literary throne. By now, though, I know better than to volunteer my own body for gestation. I have a book to finish, and a family of my own to tend. Shouldn't be too hard to find a robust grad student with towering student loans to pay off. Surely, we'll all be glad to contribute whatever we can to the creature's education. Divine spark! Never die.

(Keynote Address, Philip Roth Society, NYU, 2019)

REFUGE

ON THE FARM IN THE GREEN MOUNTAINS
BY ALICE HERDAN-ZUCKMEYER

WHEN I FIRST READ THIS wise refuge of a book, a blustering
butthole had just been elected President of the United States,
and everyone was freaking out. Via any number of platforms
on any number of screens, there was a cacophony of anxiety
and grandstanding and myopia and rage and despair such as I
have never before seen, or maybe the sheer number of platforms and screens were the never-before-seen entity. Regardless, things seemed to be turning faster and faster in some
widening gyre, to borrow a phrase from Yeats, who didn't
know the half of it. So it came to pass that I found great
comfort in the voice of Auntie Al, as I came to think of the
indomitable Alice Herdan-Zuckmayer (I can't imagine she'd
mind).

It was, in other words, just the right book at just the right
time.

Exiled from Germany at the start of World War II when the
murderous fascist dictator of the hour didn't take kindly to the
satirical critiques of her famous playwright husband ("Zuck"),
left cold by stints in New York ("We saw everything, we went
everywhere, but never found ourselves") and Los Angeles
(Zuck didn't want to write tripe for the movies), Alice and
Zuck find their way to the titular 193-acre farm in the "green
mountains" of Vermont.

These were urbane sophisticates, mind you. These were celebrated artists with connections, good clothes. These were not people who knew from farming. They had no clue if or when they might ever return "home." The very idea of "home" had become impossibly muddled, if not permanently destroyed. They were emigrants. They were immigrants. They had no choice. They had to find themselves a *new* home, and they had to get to work. They chose the farm in Vermont. They got to work.

"It was the usual course," Alice says. "One had no right to be an exception."

She refuses to be exceptional; this is one of the things that make her exceptional. There's no grandstanding here, no hand wringing, no self-pity. These twenty vignettes started out as letters to her in-laws. Updates, explanations, that's all. Practical, sensible, and "without illusion." How refreshing.

The Zuckmayers learn by necessity. They learn by doing. They acquire domestic animals (cats, dogs) and farm animals (chickens, geese, ducks, pigs, goats). They figure out feed and disease and shelter and care. They chop wood, they tend fire. They navigate dense woods and icy, snowy, muddy dirt roads. They obey the rules set forth by the seasons, the weather, the landscape, the rural community, the animals, and the land itself. They plant crops for sale and vegetables for their own sustenance. They harvest and slaughter and cook and clean. They bake and sew. They fight a harrowing infestation of rats. They take instruction from USDA pamphlets and from friendly neighbors. Farm life turns out to be a never-ending cascade of chores. Back-breaking, spirit-bending labor. But "making the best of a difficult situation" is how New Englanders live, apparently, so Auntie Al fits right in. She does the very best she can with what she has, learning as she goes. She gets by on a sense of wonder and curiosity. These are old-fashioned ideals, by which I mean essential and revolutionary. She's what my Yiddish grandmother would've called a "shtarker." A hippie before there was any such thing. Open minded and up for anything. DIY before DIY was a marketing ploy.

I fell hard for her spirit (hence the audacity of a nickname).

She has a real lot to teach us. Such as, for starters: The hardest times in life are often tangled up with the happiest. What is most difficult can be most rewarding. "Progress" is never simple or wholly positive. Sometimes when we lose, we gain, and when we gain, we lose. Our fears and joys are bound up inextricably, pleasure in pain and pain in pleasure, and our efforts to detangle and isolate human experience can leave us confused and depressed. Happiness means choosing to be productive and optimistic, recognizing despair for the ancient parasite that it is, and outsmarting it.

Alice never mentions the name of that insane murderous fascist dictator back in Germany, by the way. She barely discusses the cultural framework that enabled said murderous fascist dictator and set in motion her own exile. "The situation," she calls it. "Current circumstances." In another context this might be irritating, to say the least: call it what it is, lady! Millions upon millions of people in Europe are concurrently being systematically murdered while you wax on about the pigs and the poultry and the party line and the road conditions in Vermont! But we have a lot of literature already, don't we, about the millions upon millions, about the systematic murder. What we have less of, what we have never enough of, is literature like this: literature about what to do *instead*. Literature about embodying an alternative, creating something from nothing, inhabiting one's life fully, no matter how far circumstances deviate from expectation. Behold how, from blood and sweat and tears and toil, a livable, sustainable, eminently sane life can be forged.

"A change for the better can happen," Auntie Al muses, "a change that won't come from common sources, like the government, nor from indefinite sources, like historical developments, but can and will proceed from individuals." If there is a comforting thought to be had in these dark times (and all times are dark, are they not? Some admittedly darker than others, but I'm not in the business of relativism), surely it's this. As the sages of Pirke Avot tell us: *It is not your responsibility to finish the work of perfecting the world, but neither are you free to desist from it.* The wood always needs chopping. The furnace always needs tending. The stoves always need feeding. The goats always need milking. The floor always needs washing. Things always, always need doing, using hands and bodies, in the physical realm. Always.

"This endlessly repetitive, primitive process of accomplishment was a greater protection against care, anxiety, and fear for one's life than the application of all manner of understanding, reason, and religion," she observes. An idea whose time has come yet again, as we slowly tire of staring at never ending streams of ads and personal PR campaigns, liking, liking, loving, favoriting, liking, buying, not liking, liking, liking, liking some more, and wondering half-heartedly why everything seems at once so trite and so dire.

Resistance can take many forms. Sometimes resistance means simply turning away and busying oneself elsewhere. Think of stressed insomniac social media addicts "discovering" the Danish tradition of *hygge*, wherein it's reportedly nice to sit around the fire with loved ones, eat home-cooked meals, and talk to one another.

But as we squirm in our own dystopia, squint at dystopias past, and tremble in fear at the dystopias that lie in wait, let us not get carried away by romantic notions of the pastoral (adj: *Having the simplicity, charm, serenity, or other characteristics generally attributed to rural areas*).

"We took care of the pipes like babies, the animals like children, and the stoves like temperamental animals. Wood was sacred. We stood at the center of everything, and to survive we had to be watchman, caretaker, and protector, constantly blocking a return to chaos," Alice recalls. Nature's no warm blankie. So how was it that she managed to find in every hardship an opportunity, in every setback a gift, in every unforeseen problem an adventure, in every new obstacle a good story to tell later? Could nothing get this woman down!?

The intricacies of their days, the ins and outs of life on the farm as it is learned and lived by these unlikely inhabitants: this is superficially what *The Farm in the Green Mountains* is about. On a deeper level, it's a story of perseverance, protection, heroism, and joy. Refuge is the heart of this impossibly rich book.

The farm was Alice's refuge, and Alice's recounting of it became my own. Never mind that she's on the run from murderous fascist apes amidst a world war while I'm on the run from Facebook. And never mind the fact that behind the façade of the pastoral is the wild brutality of Nature. (Which we've worked so long and hard to dominate! So that we may now bemoan its decline! LOLZ.)

Meanwhile, Alice carries on a surprising love affair with the early Middle Ages, undertaking grueling but giddy weekly journeys to and from the Dartmouth College library so she can sit and study undisturbed by farm animals and endless chores. Just the *way* to the library, an ordeal unto itself, gets its very own chapter, immensely endearing for what it reveals about so many of us in this raggedy, time-traveling tribe of book lovers. Her ode to the library is an unexpected rapture, a sweet reprieve from farm life: "The meaning is in the books, stored up as a latent energy, and the important thing is to carry this energy over into life and make it useful to living people."

So lovingly does she speak about the library that I feel it as yet another refuge, having never set foot in it. (Although, respectfully, regarding the history and founding of the college, the "savage" Native Americans were never in need of "taming" or conversion to Christianity, but I suppose one's refuge is inevitably another's ruin.)

For a biblical seven years, the Zuckmayers live and work on the farm. Then the war is over and it's time to see what remains of the cities, friends, and relatives back "home" in Germany. They return to find unimaginable destruction, the aftermath like "tender skin that begins to grow over infected wounds." Alice isn't foolish enough to imagine that life will ever be the same. The murderous fascist elements of society "are just waiting for a new era of insanity, when crimes will again be legally permitted and the mentally ill will again achieve power and honor."

Still, the sun will rise and set. Winter will follow fall will follow summer will follow spring will follow winter. Death and decay spare no living thing; creation and destruction exist in perpetual cycles. Folksy wisdom, you might say, but don't tell me it isn't resonant when the dystopias are scratching and slobbering at the door.

There is no such thing as a long time ago in America, Alice observes at one point, and it's not hard to see why the Zuckmayers held fast to living here. Immigrants, we're told, often describe their acclimation as a kind of "second childhood." Within what is projected as the "simplicity and independence" of their adopted homeland, the Zuckmayers seem to have had a particularly happy one: "We have suffered no real disappointments, for if you accept people and things as they are you cannot be disappointed." Truth bomb, Auntie Al.

The farm is both a literal and metaphoric refuge, where the madness and brutality of a deranged world can't touch us, because we are so removed, so utterly reliant upon ourselves, and so thoroughly beholden to our work, our responsibilities. Our toil is our treasure; the landscape is our home. The best can be made of literally anything, at any time.

So the building of a new massive highway in the 1950s, when America is on its postwar progress progress progress kick, feels like a knife in the heart.

"The farm is now easy to reach," Alice informs us sadly in her postscript.

It wasn't *supposed* to be easy! It was supposed to be *hard*. Intensely, gloriously, redemptively, all-consumingly *hard*. Who came up with the idea that anything's supposed to be *easy*? Refuge is a full-time job, make no mistake. Whatever are we to do with ourselves now? Wherever can we go!?

(New York Review Books and Paris Review Daily, 2017)

SUMMER, ALBANY

THEY NEVER EMPTY the dedicated shit-can in the dog park. It's perpetually full to the brim, overflowing with poop bags, swarming with flies and wasps. Which is odd, because all the other trashcans get emptied on the regular, and the fields get mown like clockwork, every other week. Dilapidated Department of General Services' carts are often cruising around, taking care of business. So what's up with the perpetually overflowing dog park shit-can? It's the enduring mystery of summer. You can smell it from twenty feet away in the infernal heat.

I call the DGS every few days to complain about the overflowing shit-can, and always speak to the same woman. We are presumptive buds, me and the DGS lady.

"Hey, so the poop-bag thing still hasn't been dealt with."

"Yeah," she says. "Okay, gotcha. I'll let them know."

I imagine a short story I'll never write about our relationship, me and the DGS lady. About how we eventually come to share some singular kinship based on our limited exchanges. About how our different lives are ultimately defined by common struggle. Very Raymond Carver. Maybe we eventually have a fight, or a misunderstanding, or a love affair. Maybe we carry private knowledge of one another like a sacred oath, far into the future. Maybe we pass on the street and don't register a thing.

I keep getting meditation notifications on my phone from the app I downloaded months ago. *Buzz:* time to meditate. I resolutely ignore these notifications, have been ignoring them since precisely one day after I downloaded the app, but I never turn them off. To turn them off (or to delete the app altogether) would be an admission that I'm never going to meditate, and what kind of sociopath refuses to meditate? Not *me*: I *definitely* meditate. Just not right now.

Still no progress on getting the city to employ basic tools for slowing drivers and protecting pedestrians in the horrible crosswalk, though I continue to send irate letters to the City Council and neighborhood association and the Park Conservancy. I am frustrated by my impotency. All I can do is grass-roots: I have taken to waving down speeding cars.

When they slow and lower their windows, I say *Hey there, hi, hello, yes, just want to make sure you're aware that the speed limit in the park is 20! It's really scary to be a pedestrian in our public park when you're going two or three times that! Please drive safely! Thanks, have a great day!*

To which, more often than not, they respond *Go fuck yourself, you fucking bitch,* and put pedal to metal.

Just beyond the horrible crosswalk where we try daily not to die is a twenty-foot-tall monument to the eighteenth-century bard Robert Burns, National Poet of Scotland. You probably know him from "Auld Lang Syne," the New Year's Eve traditional. "Should old acquaintance be forgot," etc. (Remember Billy Crystal, doing his wildest neurotic Jew stereotype at the end of *When Harry Met Sally...? What does this song mean I don't know what this song means my whole life I been hearing this song and I don't know what this song means does it mean we should forget old friends or does it mean that we should remember old friends which is impossible because we already forgot!?*)

I think old acquaintance should most definitely be forgot, but I'm a flaming curmudgeon, somewhat willing to sustain acquaintance in "real" time/space but unwilling to sustain acquaintance in virtual time/space. It's some kind of stubborn self-abnegating bullshit. Why *not* give in to the virtual life, in all its glory? Why *not* keep abreast of everyone I've ever met, whilst forcing all of them to keep abreast of me? Why *not* banter and exchange and schmooze in virtual space, uphold the virtual discourse, make my thoughts and opinions and perspective and musings and goings-on known and known and known? I am *fine* to let old acquaintance be forgot. I wonder what Ol' Rabbie Burns would think of social media.

He was a big star, Burns was. John Steinbeck borrowed the title "Of Mice and Men" from him, Bob Dylan named "A Red, Red Rose" the most influential lyric of his life, and JD Salinger titled *Catcher in the Rye* after Holden Caulfield's misinterpretation of Burns' "Comin' Thro' the Rye." There's even a crater on Mercury named for him! Now *that's* some posterity, right there. Burns died at 37 years of age in 1796. Through his twelve children, he has over 600 living descendants as of 2012. That's a lot of ejaculate giving way to a lot more ejaculate. That's a lot of "likes." Way to go, Burns.

Near Burns is a bench we dedicated to my husband's brother Arthur, who dropped dead last year. He lived with his faithful dog on the rural tip of the Delmarva Peninsula, on the eastern shore, and was driving himself to the emergency room with chest pain when his heart expired. He very considerately steered himself off the road before he lost consciousness, because that's the kind of guy he was.

Buzz: Meditation Alert. No! Shut up, app.

The plaque on Arthur's bench bears his name and the years he lived. It says *In loving memory*. It says *Cherished brother, uncle, son, environmental scientist, and friend*. It says *A leaf on the wind*, which was sort of his mantra. Where do we want to go for dinner? Pizza, Mexican, Sushi? Everyone always jockeying for their preference, and there Arthur'd be, poised to do anything everybody else wanted. "I am but a leaf on the wind," he'd say, radiating a generally bemused expression.

A week ago, I found a flat magnet stuck to the side of the Burns monument. It pictures Osip Mandelstam's mug shot, and a quote: "Somewhere black earth holds bone / No one holds this poet's tongue."

I took the magnet. It occurred to me later that I should have left it where I found it, but it remains stuck to the radiator cover in my dining room. Do as I say, children, not as I do.

Burns is cool if you like your poets famous and flashy and fertile and memorialized in stone, but Mandelstam is more my jam: An independent thinker, at odds with his time and his government. Not a lot of "followers," in other words. He refused to toe any party line, emphasizing instead the importance of intuition and individualism. Persecuted by Stalin and sent into exile, Mandelstam froze and starved to death in a "corrective work camp" in Russia's Far East in 1938. No known descendants, but in 1977 a soviet astronomer did discover and name a minor planet after him: 3461 Mandelstam. A minor planet: That's not nothing! I can think of several ambitious contemporary poets who'd *kill* for a minor planet.

Whoever put Mandelstam on Burns must have had a good sense of humor. The more interesting poet dies alone and shivering and miserable in the prison camp. The more interesting poet is stuck like gum to the bottom of the big man's shoe. Mandelstam's mug shot is a kind of taunt, his chin lifted in defiance, like yeah, alright Burns, ya likable sellout, nice twenty-foot-tall monument, whatever, sure, cool the way millions of people usher in each new calendar year by parroting your anthem, great, whatever, but everyone knows *real* poets have to *suffer and die* in obscurity.

There's a young lady sitting on Arthur's bench today. She's cute and contemplative and I can see him there next to her, giving me a raised eyebrow and a little salute, like: *Nice setup I got here, huh?*

Arthur was not what you might call a ladies' man. On the Burns-Mandelstam continuum, he was more of a Mandelstam. He had no followers, so to speak, but his neighbors and coworkers all spoke exceptionally highly of him. To know him was to adore him. It rankles the fuck out of me that he died alone.

Hallo, dahling, I whisper. Love imagining him under the big old tree, cheerfully contemplating the horrible crosswalk where we try daily not to die.

Burns is actually kind of angled toward Arthur's bench, lost in his own contemplation, as though trying, in vain, to make sense of the vagaries of fate and fame and offspring and posterity and mortality and memory and justice.

There's been a rash of neighborhood violence. A fatal stabbing outside Lark Tavern, down the street from Ben and Jerry's. Whole block was cordoned off in the morning. Word traveled fast. The girl who owns the jewelry shop said it was self-defense: this one guy who worked at Bombers Burrito Bar was beating up his girlfriend on the regular and this other guy told him he'd better quit it, or else. So the first guy hired four dudes to beat up the second guy, who was drinking at the Tavern that night. When the four hired dudes showed up and started something, everyone got kicked out of the Tavern, so they took it to the street, where it turned out that the dude who was supposed to get beat up had a knife on him, and he stabbed the four hired brutes in self-defense. But one of the brutes died from his injuries, so now Mr. Self-Defense was in jail.

In the dog park I tell Larry the firefighter: "Hey, I'm just glad it was a good old-fashioned fatality not involving guns," and he laughs: "I know, right?" And we agree that people who don't appreciate dark humor have probably just never experienced anything truly heinous in their lives. Then we shake our heads and fall silent, staring at the overflowing shit-can.

Arthur was a superlative uncle. When he was still alive, we drew up a will and named him guardian of our kid, should we both die prematurely/simultaneously. There was no one else in the running. I still have a voicemail he left for me on our shared birthday. He spoke with a sweet lilt, articulating each syllable with special precision: *Hel-lo, E-lisa!* Why didn't I send him more kid art? Why didn't we spend every single one of our vacations down on the Barrier Islands with him? Because we just assumed there would be more time.

The animal psychic I spoke to on the phone after Sally was killed kept saying *Gee, that's a lot of loss. Gee, you've experienced a lot of loss.*

More than most, I replied, but certainly not as much as some. Don't jinx me, lady. I'm holding steady on the loss. At some point I will have had my allotment, right? And then the fates will leave me the fuck alone: isn't that how it works?

Fourth of July is like a war zone. New York State recently decriminalized fireworks for any and every yahoo, so makeshift stands and tents have sprung up all over to sell that crap. There's the usual massive official display over Empire Plaza, but ancillary explosions keep going off all night. Then there were gunshots, and it's hard to tell the difference. Six people are shot in Arbor Hill, and one stabbed. None of the people who were shot died, but the stabbing victim did die: 29 years old and a lovely guy, according to his neighbors. Two days later, another stabbing death, a couple blocks away. Massive shrine set up there now. We drive by it on our way off the highway, passing, too, as ever, all the abandoned houses and lots in Arbor Hill.

It's often posited that people go crazy in the heat. The other day a shirtless guy came sauntering through the field, sweating profusely and talking to himself whilst swinging nunchuks. *Nunchuks.* We all gave him a wide berth. Even the dogs stopped to stare. *"What the actual fuck,"* someone said.

A Lyft driver tells me *I got lots of friends in law enforcement and lemme tell you, they ain't telling us the half of what's going on around here. We don't know the half.*

There are often planes flying very low overhead. Military trainings. Airport circlings. Helicopters heading to or from Albany Med. Unsettling.

The weather *has* been weird, even for the fact that weird is now normal. Variable by thirty-degree margins, day-to-day. Dramatic passing thunderstorms, brain-fogging humidity, cicadas screaming, forty-eight-hour cold snaps, your basic angry-God stuff.

In the apartment building next door lives a couple whose industrial air conditioning unit abuts our back door. They keep it going full blast, on high dystopian roar, twenty-four hours a day, seven days a week, starting promptly on the first of June, regardless of the temperature outside.

The house on the other side used to be Robert and Alton's. Alton was a professor of theater, and Robert a professor of classics. They met at the Met Opera in the nineteen-fifties. It's difficult to imagine the realities inherent in homosexual existence seventy years ago. I can remember a bit about what it was like—the jokes, the innuendo, the teasing, the marginalization —even in relatively progressive, "tolerant" circles when I was a kid thirty years ago, and that was bad enough. When we moved in, Robert and Alton had us for dinner and gave us a wealth of children's books about Greek mythology. After Alton died, we made Robert a quiche and our small boy brought his banjo and sang a rather haunting rendition of "Where Have All The Flowers Gone?"

Robert moved out shortly thereafter. It was too much house, too many stairs, for a widower in his late eighties. At the estate sale, I scored a small painting of flowers in a gilded frame, as well as a stack of paperback autobiographies of prima ballerinas, and a framed movie poster from the 40s. Then the house sat empty for a few years. A pipe burst at one point, and water poured out of the bay window in front. A squirrel was spotted sitting in the parlor floor window another time, living the high life, sort of taunting passersby.

Now a pinched, miserable forty-something white couple are gut-renovating the place. It will become their "dream house," they tell us, then cease communicating altogether. There's a horrible racket every day from dawn til dusk, an endlessly rotating cast of the cheapest contractors in town, and a thick dusting of demolition debris (or as I like to call it: cancer) all over our garden and deck. We're trying not to despise them, but it's a daily struggle.

BUZZ: time to meditate.

A steamy thunderstorm descends, and in the aftermath the shit-bag situation is like a hearty, simmering shit-stew, so I call my girl at the DGS yet again, and leave another message.

"Hey babe," I say, because we're intimates, of a sort. "How's it going? Wondering about that shit-can. And by the way, unrelated, FYI, the flag's still at half-mast." (They lowered it when Barbara Bush died, then seem to have forgotten about it.)

"Nxivm" is all over the news, some creepy-ass cult situation getting national coverage for the faintest whiff of minor celebrity involvement. Far-flung friends mention it to me on the regular. Hey, how 'bout that Albany cult! It's the only time anyone reads about Albany in national news. It *is* very Albany, this cult, what with the office parks and day-spas in mini-malls and obsession with the faintest whiff of minor celebrity and female-branding ceremonies in suburban McMansion basements and whatnot. Or maybe what I mean by "Albany" is "America."

When we lived in Europe we met lots of people who are bonkers mad crazy in love with the idea of America. They drive Route 66 on their honeymoons and wear t-shirts emblazoned with Miami / Detroit / LasVegas / Venice Beach / Brooklyn / Nashville / Chicago / NYC / Seattle. When they come visit us they want to gawk at the urban ruins, the abandoned houses, the oldest building in the state of New York, which stands (abandoned) alongside an expansive parking lot under a pointless, deteriorating highway. They are hypnotized by how careless and wasteful we are, how we discard everything, including our own history, and just plow heedlessly ahead. How we have so much *space*, so much endless freaking *room* to just throw away and throw away and start again. A ruined city, an abandoned mess of a city? No problem, to hell with it, build a new suburb, a new subdivision, a new mall, a new supermarket, new gas stations, new highways. We can just keep going like this forever, can't we??

I spent a half hour the other day driving around this nearby office park called "Corporate Woods," looking for its huge sign to photograph and post on Insta. *This would be funny*, I intended to caption it, *if it were a MOTHERFUCKING JOKE*. But I couldn't find the sign. Could've sworn I'd driven by it before, but it was like the Bermuda Triangle in there, so eventually I gave up and got the hell out while the gettin was good.

Today a huge Doberman with intact balls named Charleston comes over to where I'm sitting in the grass, lifts his leg, and takes a generous piss all over me. There is wet warmth seeping down my back before I understand what's happening. I'm enraged. I'm not just pissed *off*, I say, to make my kid laugh, I'm pissed *on*. Charleston's owner is fifty yards away, chatting obliviously on her phone.

"Teach your dog some fucking manners," I mutter as I head home to take a shower, my swell sundress soaked in dog urine.

And now, great, here comes a furiously scowling landlady from around the block. She owns the building where the A/C freaks live. Not sure why she hates me, but I am more than capable of coming up with reasons to hate myself, so how can I blame her? Probably she hates me because last year, when we had to go halfsies on the falling-down old fence between our yards, I physically blocked her contractor from chain-sawing all to shit the huge root of the enormous healthy beautiful maple on the property line. I delivered an impassioned speech on behalf of the tree, appealing first to common sense (*Haven't you read The Lorax!?*), then to spirituality (*This tree is older than your grandmother's grandmother's grandmother!*) and then, when neither inspired mercy, to crass materialism (*Our property values are dependent on the presence of beautiful old trees like this one!*).

I hate trees, said the contractor in his thick Russian monotone, and the landlady scowled so hard I thought her face might burst into flames and melt right off, but the tree was left to live.

"Hello," I say. Something has come over me. I am dripping Doberman piss. I do not want to be at odds with my neighbors! Life is too short! "I'm wondering if I've wronged you in some way," I say, "because you seem very angry with me, and I'm really sorry if I've done you wrong."

"I think we have different *personalities*," she says, and keeps walking.

"Have a beautiful day!" I call after her. Yes, darling, I should rather hope that we have different personalities.

Buzz: meditate. Shut up! Fuck off!

For a while, in the wake of Arthur's disappearance from the material world, my kid became obsessed with curating a playlist in memoriam. *Arthur's Funirol*, he titled it. "My Heart Will Go On" from *Titanic*, "Somewhere Over the Rainbow" as sung by the Hawaiian dude with the ukulele, a maudlin cover of "Hey Hey, My My," the folk classic "Fare Thee Well (Dink's

Song)," Coldplay's "Everglow"... Each and every track is a killer. We listen to it every day.

After Arthur's memorial service, a relative held forth on how to talk to children about death: "Tell them the truth," he shrugged.

"Oh?" I said. "And what is that, pray tell?" I was excited to learn, at long last, the Truth About Death.

"That there's nothing," he said. "It's The End!"

I laughed in his face. "Wow," I said. "How *super-duper cool* that you know that! How like totally *incredible* that you know that."

I prefer to tell my kid a different truth. Ready for it? It's pretty intense. It might fuck you up. Here it is: I don't know.

Then one day the guy who runs the homeless shelter gets stung by a wasp while trying to toss yet another shit-bag onto the overflowing shit-can pile, and it becomes clear that the reason the dedicated shit-can is never emptied is because it is bolted to the stake upon which it stands, so to empty it one must reach inside it to pick up handfuls of shit-bags at a time. No wonder it is never emptied! Who gets paid enough to empty a dog park shit-can by reaching into it!? Come on. Odell Beckham Jr. doesn't get paid enough to empty a shit-can a handful at a time.

So to my DGS sister I now say: "How about we just remove the thing entirely? Seems like kind of a design flaw, huh?"

"I'll let them know, hon," she says. "Gotcha. Thanks."

An archaic Jewish law holds that if a husband dies and the husband has an available brother, the widow should marry that brother.

"I know how fucked up this sounds," I tell my husband, "but if you had died, I would have been totally fine to marry Arthur." But here's the weirdest thing: losing Arthur seems to have deepened and strengthened our own bond. Even in death, that guy makes everything better for everyone.

I have his big heavy grey VIRGINIA sweatshirt. And a small clay hamsa strung on two inches of red leather, which used to hang by his back door. And one of those fundamentalist Christian fish symbols with "Gefilte" written inside of it, meant to stick to the back of your car. (I used to have the same exact one on the back of my first car, a baby blue '86 Volvo wagon.) And some of his DVDs: *Harry Potter, Monty Python, Young Franken-stein, Spaceballs*. Also *Must Love Dogs*, a 2005 rom-com. Why did he own *Must Love Dogs*!? I finally watch it one night, because he liked it. It's about loneliness, missed chances, misunderstand-ings, ships passing in the night, and finally, happy-ever-after.

I know it's easy to idealize the dead, but he really was the best. Words fail. A *mensch*, which is Yiddish (and German) for human being, a person of dignity and honor. He was a mensch's mensch. He was a mensch's mensch's mensch. He offered and engendered gladness. Glad, meaning pleased, delighted. From the old English "glaed," meaning bright, shin-ing. Before that, Old Norse: "glathr," meaning bright, joyous. Before that, German: "glatt," smooth. And before *that*, the Latin "glaber," meaning hairless. Isn't language a trip?

The sunsets are golden and pink and orange and shim-mering now, at the height of summer. In the amphitheater they're doing a run of *Damn Yankees* followed by a run of *How to Succeed in Business Without Really Trying*.

Tons of people in the park at magic hour. A man from the group home on Lancaster comes to play with the dogs. A young state worker in a suit who can occasionally be convinced to play soccer with my kid. Chaim, a Kabbalist, wearing his Aleph hat. Koresh an Iranian who uses a wheel-chair and loves soccer and dabbles in ceramics. Jim, who spent 40 years in the CIA and was "Billy" Clinton's frat brother at Georgetown. Laura the pharmacy student. A dozen dogs named Luna. Why are all the dogs named Luna? Same reason a lot of the Caucasian babies born in Texas in 2015 were named Emma or Mason, I guess. Groupthink. Suggestibility. Collec-tive unconscious.

Buzz: time to meditate! Great idea, that. Next time, for sure.

If Arthur's seems like too short a life, that's kind of greedy thinking, isn't it? In like two or three measly generations we've come to feel entitled to a hundred years, or bust. Fifty is a fairly respectable life span, in the scope of human existence. Anyway: entitlements are such a stupid fucking bore.

It's early August when they finally empty the dog park shit-can. "They:" a DGS guy with a grabber-arm thing-a-ma-jig. He painstakingly removes piles of fermented soupy summer dog shit, and everyone nearby bursts into spontaneous applause.

A week later it's full again. But by the end of the month, they remove the shit can entirely, and I wonder if I dreamed up the whole thing. Like maybe there was never any shit-can bolted to a stake there at all. But look, the grass is scarred, so it must have been real.

"Hey hon," I tell DGS lady's voicemail. "It's gone! Thanks for your help. See you around."

A stranger on a bike in the park stops to chat with me in twilight, after all the other dogs and people have gone home.

"Hello," he says. I look at him like wtf dude. Is he going to stab or shoot me? He's got a British accent. We have a completely innocuous conversation, but he seems to know me.

"Keep up your writing," he says. And when he rides off again I am overtaken by the brief conviction that he was God. I may have been a little stoned.

On the first of October, when the high is 62 degrees, the A/C freaks next door finally, finally power it down, and there is a week of quiet before the leaf blowers begin.

I never get around to turning off the meditation notifications. Fall and another winter and another spring and another summer will pass, and I'll keep on ignoring that damn app, in spite of its (and my?) better intentions.

(Longreads, 2019)

POOR ELISA

ON LA FEMME DE GILLES BY MADELEINE BORDOUXHE

IT'S PROBABLY NOT unusual to read a novel whose protagonist bears your own name if your name is Jane or Emily or John or Jack, but it's a neat first for me. What immediate force of recognition! Elisa: a tall, handsome woman, breasts not as high and mighty as once they were, fully vested in domestic life, and holding fast to the hope that domestic life *matters*, because breasts, like time, only go in one direction. Cry us a river.

But Madeleine Bordouxhe's Elisa—the novel's centerpiece, marginalized from the get-go by its clever title—is massively betrayed by her cheerfully unrepentant husband on page 11. And Bourdouxhe's Elisa can't skip off to an artist's colony and seek revenge with a neurotic sculptor or hop a train down to the city and buy a new dress and flirt with someone at a party, or take the kids to live in an intentional community in Vermont, where she'd discover an affinity for orgies and hallucinogens and spinning pottery (as this Elisa might). Bourdouxhe's Elisa—known in her own damn novel as *Gilles' Woman*, for god's sake—has no recourse. No practical recourse, and worse, no emotional recourse. There's no precedent for middle-aged feminist reinvention in pre-WWII-era rural/industrial Belgium (that I know of).

So here we have a sad novel about a sad lady, very matter-of-fact in its cadences. The sentences unfurl in an even tone. The chapters are brief and eventful. Elisa is very, very sad, and for good reason. She is a sad salad sandwich on toasted sad. She is in torment, and she does the only thing she knows how to do: she waits it out.

We know everything there is to know about sad women. Our formative education was likely full of them (as, for that matter, are our moms' groups, book clubs, bridal showers, and girls' nights out). We're X-ray clear on misdirected loyalties and squandered selves. We know the sad-lady drill: selfless, devoted, doing the best she can. She has limited choices and no options, or no options she's aware of, which is the same thing. What would happen if she were to attempt to break free, grasp at independence or some authentic expression of self? She'd wind up under a literal or metaphorical train, of course. Anyway, what would "freedom" even *look* like? Don't be ridiculous. She's fine. No, no, really, she's *fine*.

Did I mention that Bourdouxhe's Elisa is expecting her third child? And that her husband is fucking her sister? Yeah, she's got it pretty bad. But the worst part is that Elisa doesn't *blame* her husband (or sister, who is described, viciously and perfectly, as "one of those women who just *knows*" the minute they've snared any man's attention). The truly terrible part is that Elisa remains completely, utterly besotted by Gilles, regardless. The totally awful part is that she only wants him back, and she is prepared to quietly hold her ground for as long as it takes until he grows tired of the affair. No kicking, no screaming, no recrimination or sulking: Elisa soldiers on. She makes breakfast. She cares for the children. She cleans the kitchen. She sweeps the steps.

Let's talk about domestic heavy-lifting, why don't we: keeping the home-fires burning, loving unreservedly and endlessly, negating ourselves in the service of those we love, and maybe even managing to take some form of quotidian joy in it all. These things cannot yet be done by robots; hopefully will *never* be handed entirely over to robots. And a working-class woman like Elisa can't hire other women to do it for her.

And the gendered lineage of this work (yes: work) cannot be wiped away by declarative intent or starry-eyed idealism. Elisa's understanding of her burdens is one of the novel's triumphs, and her only solace. She experiences a "deep sense of pride, untouched by scorn, rising within her and comforting her soul." Yes, caring for other people is important. Gilles and his childish lust are nothing compared to Elisa's elemental, necessarily *female* knowledge of this fact.

Or so I noted in the margins before I put the manuscript aside to go prepare dinner for my family.

In her stellar afterword, translator Faith Evans talks about some of the pinnacles of sorrowful literary womanhood that preceded *La Femme de Gilles*, but I'd rather look forward for comparison, into a future Bourdouxhe's Elisa couldn't possibly imagine: Nora Ephron's *Heartburn*.

Similarly betrayed by her adored husband, Ephron's pregnant protagonist refuses to stay put. She dynamites their life, tells all their friends, moves out, and spends the rest of the novel riffing hilariously on romance, identity, culture, sex, love, family, food, and money. *Heartburn*'s opening line reads almost like a cruel summation of *La Femme de Gilles*: "The first day I did not think it was funny." But then, wonder of wonders, Ephron's narrator goes on: "I didn't think it was funny the third day, either, but I managed to make a little joke about it."

A joke! Perhaps the canniest, quickest way to defy expectations about the wronged woman. A joke: the easiest, cleverest way for a wronged woman to empower herself. Here are two parallel heartbroken women half a century apart, both thrown away like garbage. One will be okay in the end, and one will not. The difference is in the ability to make a little joke. If only Elisa had it in her!

Nothing's wrong with sadness, mind you. Sadness is crucial. Sadness is an important and profitable base layer. Sadness is necessarily step one. It can lead to many interesting places, like, for example, anger, absurdity, self-awareness, lust, maybe even (dare to dream) *change*. And humor. Blessed, life-saving humor. Ephron understood this, so her narrator skips along, setting off land mines and giggling maniacally. *Heartburn*'s narrator is a many-armed goddess of recrimination, rage, perversity, and laughter. Her story is hers to tell, and her telling is, itself, a perfect fulfillment of the chaotic emotional wreckage therein. She rises like a phoenix from the ashes.

But Ephron was a different kind of woman, living in a different era. A half-century elapsed between the setting of *La Femme de Gilles* and that of *Heartburn*. (Almost exactly as long on the other end, incidentally, as between *Anna Karenina* and *La Femme de Gilles*.) Something must have opened up the heavens during that half-century to pave the way for the possibility of a woman having the last laugh. Historians and sociologists and journalists have different ideas about what this something was. Maybe it was the atom bomb.

What makes *La Femme de Gilles* achingly contemporary and urgently relevant, is its stark portrayal of sadness as a dead end. Elisa swallows the wrongs enacted upon her and then, well. What do you think happens to a person without access to rage, perversity, absurdity, self-awareness, or humor? A specifically female person, to whom the luxuries of rage and perversity and self-awareness and humor have been denied as a matter of course? It's like trying to scream in a dream and being unable to make a sound.

"Deprived of the feeling that she must act... [Elisa] gained the shattering liberty of looking things in the face."

Look things in the face she sure does, turning around and around in place, one foot nailed to the floor, hoping very hard that somehow, somehow, her domestic bliss might be redeemed, intact. She's no coward, she just doesn't know that rage and humor and lust are options. And how would she?

Gilles wants to "stake his claim on life," while Elisa "cannot conceive of any greater happiness than giving him pleasure." It'd be easy to say okay, sure: so he's a jerk/man and she's a pathetic woman. But reducing it to a gender binary misses the point. Gilles is not an asshole because he wants to assert his vitality via his genitals; Gilles is an asshole because Elisa doesn't fully exist for him. Elisa is not weak because she enjoys giving her husband pleasure; Elisa is weak because she does not fully exist for herself.

The mother of a friend once gave me the following advice: Marry someone who loves you just a *little bit* more than you love him. (She said this in a whisper, so her devoted husband wouldn't hear.) You give so much of yourself in a marriage, she was implying, and there is ultimately so little accounting for the psychic economy therein, that it's a good idea to cover your ass, as it were, with a surfeit of adoration. As marriage advice goes, it's not entirely without merit, though upon reflection it does sound like giving yourself permission to be a creep.

Anyway, it's 1930 and there are boy soldiers crawling through the grass outside her window, rehearsing their own doom. Bourdouxhe's Elisa can't write a think piece about having been betrayed, parlay it into a book deal, and promote it via Instagram with a chic, aspirational rural/industrial aesthetic. And alas, psychiatric meds haven't yet been invented.

I read *La Femme de Gilles* as a cautionary tale, as riveting as any contemporary "It Happened to Me." We *still* like our women self-abnegating. Self-blaming. Self-whatevering. Self-fill-in-the-blank-ing (just not self-pleasuring, hell no). Placid, at any rate. Or maybe, *maybe*, just kind of mewling prettily over in a corner. We *still* like our women woman enough to bear their suffering stoically, silently, heroically. We still prefer that women not *bother* us with their suffering. Even—or especially —when said suffering has been foisted upon them. Even and especially when they have been expressly hurt, violated, betrayed. Embroidering shame about having been wronged is just so *pretty*. We trade on that, call it "likable."

"What she needed was help in reconstructing her life on earth, someone to comfort her." No dice, Elisa. We are the closest she'll get. We readers, witnesses. And aren't *we* also "Gilles' women?" Aren't *we* subject to him, too? As we bear witness to this saga, align ourselves with poor Elisa and, as captive audience to her paralysis, helplessly watch her perish?

No one will say that Bourdouxhe's Elisa is "unlikable," because folks dumb enough to still be having that kind of conversation *love* them some sorrowful silence, one foot nailed to the floor, maybe just a pinch of mewling for flavor. Dare to raise the mewling to a moan, a dirge, or, heaven forbid, a scream? Crazy bitch, get on some meds.

Ask yourself, when you read this novel, whether or not you "like" Elisa. Ask yourself *why* you like her, or why you do not. Do you like her because she is stoic and uncomplaining? Do you like her because she downplays her heartache? Do you like her because you pride yourself on being this way, too? Do you like her because she's a victim of circumstance, because she has been wronged? Do you like that? What do you do when you are wronged? Do you swallow it? Are you faithful to the status quo? Do you blame yourself? Are you very, very sad? Do you let people see that? Do you ever wake up screaming from a nightmare but find you're actually just barely grunting?

Or do you dislike Elisa? Do you dislike her because she is impotent, paralyzed? Does that frustrate you? Do you dislike her because she has no recourse, no options? What is your recourse? What are your options?

"The smell of suffering always disgusts others," Elisa observes. *La Femme de Gilles* is a detailed portrait of the very worst kind of suffering there is: submerged, denied, and dutifully ignored.

Were Elisa to burn down her literal or metaphorical house, maybe the novel would boast a happy ending. Were she able to make a real ugly scene, maybe a new beginning would await her on the other side of misery. But we have always preferred a woman who does nothing to enact her own humanity. A woman who punishes herself, even when she's not to blame. We prefer it this way because it's simpler this way. It's how she purifies herself, see? She is a closed circuit, like the novel itself. Sure, the price she pays is her very *self*, but at least our sympathy can remain intact. And isn't sympathy, after all, Elisa's most important currency? Her *only* currency? Sad woman here! Come and get yer sad woman! She's *paralyzed* with sorrow, folks. She's got no support! Her only option is to bear it alone, silently, until she can bear it no more! Saaaaad woman, here! Come and get some suuuuuper sad wo-*man*!

If she were to turn feral—like Ephron's narrator, who finally, at a polite party, smashes a pie in the philanderer's face —we must, on some level, censure her, shake our heads and cluck our disapproval, even as we smirk, and even as we probably envy her that wild freedom and self-possession. You can't go around smashing pies in people's faces.

La Femme de Gilles oversteps not one single boundary. Elisa defies not one single expectation. Her torment is exquisitely private and dignified and profoundly feminine, a secret dutifully kept. Can't she run off with that frisky soldier who winks at her from the meadow? Can't she cast off the bonds of housewifery, if only for an hour, a day? Can't she publicly shame Gilles? Can't she slap the smug smile off her little sister's face? Can't she plunge a hot poker through Gilles' lame excuse for a heart!? Can't she dump some of that delicious soup she's forever making down his pants?

(No, she cannot.)

And we, for our part, can only read to find ways of *contextualizing*. It was a different time, we remind ourselves. Well, yes and no. If Elisa were to "stand up" for herself, she'd lose sympathy, and a woman who doesn't have sympathy has nothing, nothing, nothing at all.

So Elisa keeps it under wraps. All her torment, all her shame. All her heartbreak, none of it her doing. She's *such* a good woman. She carefully spares her friends and neighbors the unpleasantness of her own devastation. How considerate. The novel has the unhappiest of endings, but it can at least still be said that Elisa exits her narrative intact, because we get to feel unremittingly, sorry for her. *We* get to be outraged on her behalf, which makes *us* all-powerful, and who doesn't want to be all-powerful? Certainly not poor Elisa, never fear. What a lovely, relatable woman. Just how we like 'em. Patient and uncomplaining and... Well. You can probably guess where she's headed.

"Just wait," the narrative exhorts her as the novel barrels toward its shattering conclusion. "Don't give up on yourself, just wait!"

But Elisa is finally, finally done waiting. She has exhausted her impressive reserves of patience. There is no relief. I feel her pain. But I confess I wished I could butt in and put a pie in Gilles' face, myself, to try and offer poor Elisa the simple and possibly saving grace of a laugh.

(Melville House, and Paris Review Daily, 2017)

ANI-FESTO

A FOLKSINGER IS a voice of and for the people, the implication being that not all people have the insight, energy, or freedom to speak or sing for themselves. A folksinger is special only insofar as she is blessed with that insight, energy, and freedom, in spades, and willing to devote her life to giving voice. A folksinger doesn't need a fancy institutional education or the approval of gatekeepers. A folksinger doesn't have to be connected or privileged or attractive or aspirational or anointed in any way. A folksinger needs neither permission nor anything so mythical or subjective as innate "talent." A folksinger doesn't even need a "good" voice. A folksinger barely even needs an official audience, let alone a manager, promoter, tour bus, or sound engineer (though all those things probably come in handy).

All a folksinger needs is guts, heart, soul, and the dedication to work her ass off, indefinitely. And, oh: a lack of vanity, which is arguably the rarest ingredient of all.

Cut to your garden-variety sensitive/suicidal teenaged freak coming of age in the 1990s amidst a swirl of mass-marketed female voices: Natalie Merchant, Erykah Badu, Alanis Morissette, Meshell Ndegeocello, Jewel, Sarah McLachlan, Tracy Chapman, Liz Phair, Lauryn Hill. I adored them indiscriminately. My cultural discernment in its earliest evolutionary stages was rather... loose, music being the ultimate refuge, though I'm glad I never went to Lilith Fair.

The teacher appears when the student is ready. Enter, a mix tape.

There was Ani's captivating lullaby "Both Hands," and her gentle instructional "Fire Door," and her ferocious insistence to "Anticipate," and the rallying cry of "Names and Dates and Times," and the insouciant "Blood in the Boardroom," and then the hard realism of "Willing to Fight." Holy shit: DiFranco, barely out of her own teens, stomped into my consciousness and left her singular boot prints all over the place. She sang of love and friendship and easy lies and hard truths and adventure and self-reliance and sex and romance and struggle. I needed her, bad.

How much of mainstream music (or art, or writing, for that matter), past and present, amounts to: Like me! Love me! Agree with me! Fuck me! Pay me! Imitate me! Worship me! Obey me! Follow me! Fuck me some more! Adore me! Pay me some more! I'm rich! Did I mention how rich I am? Sooooo rich! Check out my outfit! Like me!

Ani was different. Ani embodied the idea that you could *resist* what was proscribed for you in any given context, and you could have unpopular or idiosyncratic or wildly unheard-of perspectives, and *you could share them*. And dance and growl and stomp and bounce and shout and giggle all the while. The process of figuring shit out could be *fun*. And hey! While you're at it, refuse categorization, refuse definition, refuse to play by anyone else's rules. Refuse complicity in your own cultural degradation. And even though you'll probably be mocked, sometimes threatened, mostly ignored, and occasionally punished, no one can actually stop or silence you, so long as you draw the breath of life. Overthrowing existing power structures doesn't have to be a *drag*. Revolution can be a fucking *party*.

She was the first truly unafraid woman I ever saw or heard. Not a trace of timidity. No hesitation or self-negation. No prim, apologetic requests for permission. No self-serious protesting-too-much. Hey, her songs said, lend me your ears. I am worthy of your attention for this passing moment. I am hard to ignore, but I won't waste your time.

A manifesto is a public declaration of principles, policies, or intentions, especially of a political nature. Try this one on for size: Ani DiFranco is the greatest living folksinger of the post-Dylan era, and the only reason most people don't give much of a crap is because she is a woman.

That guitar in her hands, so fast and fluent and percussive, like an extra limb! It sounded, I realized when I began to write stories and essays, exactly like the kind of stop-time typing or scribbling I did when I didn't have to pause to ponder what I *really* thought and felt, or whether it was "acceptable" to think and feel what I really thought and felt, or whether *others* might react badly to what I really thought and felt. Freedom, in other words! Fearlessness. Authority. Expertise. Don't waste your cash on creative retreats with ego-disordered internet person-alities; just pay attention to the work of artists who function as mediums, and who, as such, don't need your adulation or approval. See if you can disconnect your *own* ego, with its obnoxious tsk-tsk-ing, its political maneuvering, its fear mongering and mirror-checking and jockeying, long enough to make something authentic enough to be worth your *own* time, let alone anyone else's.

Ani was alternately manic, intimate, delicate, gorgeous, furious. Her voice veered from whisper to growl to twang to spoken word and back again, sometimes in the span of a single verse. She played her instrument like it (and she) was on fire. A lot of my friends hated her, thought her voice "annoying." I tried and tried to explain that they were missing the point, but nobody enjoys being lectured about why they're wrong about music (or art or politics or writing), so I found new friends.

I stood there at I-don't-know-how-many shows in my imitative steel-heeled boots, with my imitative waist-length hair extensions courtesy of twelve hours at an illegal storefront salon in Waltham, Mass. A comrade in the balcony once took a photo of me standing up against the stage, at Ani's feet. You can't see my face, but I'm sure it was tear streaked. I screamed myself silly at those shows. Memorized every lyric, every beat, every in-joke, every variation in phrasing. Those were the *Living in Clip* years, with Andy Stochansky on drums and Sara Lee on bass. There was joy and resistance and an energy I can't adequately describe except to say that it was spiritual, it made the hell of surviving puberty seem completely fucking worth it, I was finally cured of pretending I liked the taste of other people's shit, and I no longer wanted to kill myself.

She began playing guitar at nine, having made an unlikely friend in the Buffalo musician/promoter/folk hero Michael Meldrum, some thirty years her senior. She was legally emancipated at fifteen ("born into a family built like an avalanche"), dropped out of high school, and toured relentlessly, living on the road. She studied poetry at The New School, occasionally sleeping at Port Authority. Soon enough industry scouts came knocking, but she was wary, and carried on, on her own. For a long while she survived by selling cassette tapes on the road. She refused to sell t-shirts for years. At 19, with the help of her sometimes-boyfriend Scot Fisher, she formed Righteous Babe Records, on which she put out her first record and the 21 studio albums (two of which are collaborations with storyteller Utah Phillips), four live albums (excluding dozens of bootlegs), two compilation albums, and three extended plays (so far!) that followed.

And she remained in full control of her own work, which is what has become the dominant narrative of DiFranco: giggly petite weirdo dyke freak from Buffalo with the guitar and the fucked-up hair who started her own record label, The End. The independent label, the total control: this is the story with which DiFranco's notoriety tends to start and stop: not *just* some freak dyke whatever-the-hell with a guitar, mind you, but an *entrepreneurial* freak dyke whatever with a guitar. Color mainstream culture *impressed*.

In her epic 1998 open letter to *Ms.* magazine, Ani had had enough of being That-Girl-With-Her-Own-Record-Label. The magazine had included DiFranco in its list of "21 Feminists for the 21st Century" but its explication of her importance focused solely on her business acumen, particularly the fact that she made "more money per album sold than Hootie and the Blowfish." Even the supposed feminist media mothership couldn't or wouldn't frame a folk/punk hero's accomplishments as anything other than a capitalist triumph.

DiFranco's blistering letter burned that bullshit to the ground. "All of my achievements are artistic, as are all of my failures," she wrote. "I'll bust ass for 60 people, or 6,000, watch me."

"No sooner had the media finally embraced me than I was having trouble with the *way* they embraced me," DiFranco jokes in her 2019 memoir, *No Walls and the Recurring Dream.*

Spin offered her some free ad space early on, because they dug what she was doing, but the ad she submitted read, simply, "EAT PUSSY NOT COWS," and Spin declined to run it. When invited, some years later, to appear on Letterman, she declared her intention to sing "Subdivision," a brutally insightful song about the racism inherent in twentieth century American urban planning. The Letterman folks politely requested "something a little more upbeat." DiFranco refused, was disinvited, and never invited back.

We live in a culture obsessed with labels, fame, marketing, numbers, and money. We volunteer for mass behavior modification; our tools for counting and enforcing evolve and become ever more sophisticated. We speak now, without irony, with *admiration*, of who has the most "followers." Can the true spirit of punk ever withstand the rigors and vagaries of international fame? Can singularity of voice and vision ever survive the "success" of canonization within popular culture? The early self-annihilation of some of our purest—Holiday, Joplin, Winehouse, etc. ad nauseum—suggest not. The ones who live long and prosper within the industry? They tend to play by the rules, though they may make perfunctory aesthetic gestures toward rebellion.

Perhaps the only way for an artist to survive as such is to fight off mainstream success and recognition, insist upon doing things the hard way, the lonely way, the uphill way. In other words: avoid getting insanely rich and insanely famous. (Cue "Joyful Girl.") "One thing's for sure," Ani writes in *No*

Walls: "fame ain't gonna make a people person of you if you don't dig people already."

She calls bullshit absolutely everywhere and is absolutely freaking right about absolutely freaking everything. She is resolutely uncategorizable and unmarketable, never sticking to any particular aesthetic long enough to be commodified as its representative. Shaved head, extensions, dreads, blue hair styled with glue, nose ring, chest tat... her "look" is never the point. And yet, and yet: *Rolling Stone's* coverage of *No Walls and the Recurring Dream,* a profile/interview in the year of our Lord 2019, opens with the following query: "Will Ani DiFranco wear a dress?" And a few years back, *The Hairpin* ran a witty piece by two self-identified "millennial" "lesbians" subtitled "An Inquiry into the Non-Legacy of Ani DiFranco," a wildly ageist misfire, with extra points for profound ignorance on the subjects of maternal politics and identity, perimenopause, and (projected) sexual orientation. The gist was that DiFranco is just, like, *old* and, too, like, presumptively heterosexually monogamous to matter. Also: she's a *mom* now, and who could *possibly* want to hear someone's *mom* grappling with her *humanity*? Gross!

The people I see most loudly broadcasting socially progressive hashtaggery, who are most proud of their pseudo-feminist-slogan t-shirts and pink hats at protest marches, who are *most* insistent that their children *also* wave protest signs and wear slogan t-shirts, who were the *most* shocked and outraged and sort of spiritually *disabled* by the ascendancy of the 45th President of The United States, and who refuse even the most basic responsibility for understanding their own reproductive biology... are almost invariably the very same people who, back in college, used to roll their eyes at DiFranco, joke about hairy-legged man-haters, ditch their friends the nanosecond a dude came sniffing around, and say shit like "I'm not a *feminist* or anything, but I *am* pro-choice" or "I'm not a *feminist* or anything, but rape isn't cool." I *remember* you, folks. I was *there,* taking notes. "Isn't she one of those angry dykes with a guitar?" I still occasionally hear someone wonder. Live long enough and you start to see the most fascinating reversals. Aging is both a profound privilege and a deeply disorienting burden.

We all love to pretend that when we finally do grasp large-scale injustice and perversity, we are simply emerging fully formed into an enlightenment that is our birthright. *Obviously* we are awake to racism, to sexism, to the destruction, for profit, of the earth and all its inhabitants. *Obviously* we are enraged at the systemic oppressions and power abuses that characterize every human society in history. We are so eager to forget our own complicities and blindness. We are forgetful of our own historic failures to call out injustice until a tidal wave of popular opinion carries us effortlessly along on its swell, when we are glad to pretend we emerged fully formed into the progressive stances that should have been innate all along.

But progressive movements do not spring, fully formed, from the minds and bodies of some magical collective consciousness. Lineage and struggle, from the ground up, is the story of any progressive movement, any positive human movement whatsoever.

I'm not trying to convince you to accept Ani DiFranco as your personal savior; Jews are not allowed to proselytize, and there's nothing to be said about Ani the folksinger, Ani the renegade, Ani the music industry outlier, Ani the activist, Ani the performer, or Ani the lyricist that will convince you, if you've already dismissed her, to reassess. "I don't argue where there's real disagreement," wrote Grace Paley. But to any haters who've somehow read this far: You're missing out on a shit-ton of fun, and you're probably carrying around a massive shitload of unexamined internalized misogyny, too.

There have been outliers and rebels and true folkie punks speaking to us for ages, telling us how it is, begging us to listen, to hear, to look, to see. That it often takes us so long to hear is what's amazing. Folk music is elemental political activism, progress is a process, and the ethos of any truly progressive movement or consciousness must always privilege process over product.

Even the best of us can be blind, but Ani's been clear-eyed for as long as I can remember. Feminism, civil and human rights, #MeToo, climate change, gun control, reproductive justice, globalization, mass media brainwashing, racism, the politics of suburbia, queer identity, name it: Ani has a searing lyric about it from before most of you were born. Is it anti-intellectual to say that I learned everything I know about every kind of social justice from this "little folksinger"? Long live DiFranco. The kicker being that she doesn't *want* to be a public face of folk wisdom or punk business models or anything of the sort. She wants to find the funny absurd unjust tragic inane insanities of life and love and she wants to play us a couple songs.

Around her brass band era, after *Little Plastic Castle*, I took a break from Ani super-fandom, though I was never wholly indifferent. I kept abreast. I caught her live whenever possible. But we both had a lot of shit to figure out, me and Ani, and it was important we go our separate ways for a while.

Then there I was, feeling dazed and unsupported on the other side of childbirth, and there she was with *Red Letter Year*, also on the other side of childbirth, and she sounded as exultant and proud and scared as I felt, and softer, and more vulnerable, her energies redirected in new and radical ways. I was trying to learn how to not fuck up marriage and mother-hood, and there was this one refrain on one of the many earnest love songs—the downright *uncomfortably* earnest love songs—on *Which Side Are You On?* that shook me: *It took me a long... time... to... find... love.*

She doesn't attack her guitar the way she used to; doesn't growl and stutter and stomp the way she used to. Remember what an animal she was onstage with that guitar? Hilarious, all-in. "Gonna play you another one from the bad old days," she said onstage at a show recently. "Ah, yes, the bad old days." She laughed that deep-belly open-jawed laugh of hers. "Isn't it nice not to be running around all psycho anymore because of *this*?" She gestured somewhat violently in the direction of her pelvis. She's changed. She's gotten gentler. It's so moving, because it's a precious and rare model of a way to age. (Cue "If Yr Not": *if you're not getting happier as you get older... you're fucking up*")

These days she plays like someone who has come a very long way on foot.

You can't keep a good woman down, as the old (meaningless) saying goes, though lord knows there have been untold successful attempts to keep a great many good women down. Maybe what that saying really means is that power is greater than any one individual, and that while many are indeed crushed—spiritually and politically and corporeally speaking—we can always take solace in the knowledge that some voices will nevertheless break through, blaze into being, and find sufficient airspace into which they can sing, talk, exhort, shout, rage, whisper, hum, counter, protest.

There is another way, these voices coherently assure us. *Come with me.* We need these voices like we need air, food, water, touch; they sustain us through lives beset with injustice, violence, condescension, silence, theft, and lies. These voices don't tend to have a hundred, a thousand, ten thousand voices chanting their names, hollering assent, but the trade-off is that these voices remain *free*, see? And freedom is worth the long road.

"There's no me without you," Ani said at another recent show. "And there's no you without me. So we need each other. We actually need each other or none of this is real."

Don't get me wrong: I liked my share of corporate pop hits *when I was a child*, but then my frontal lobe fully fucking developed, and though I'm still glad to rock out to some bullshit at a karaoke bar or on a long car ride, and though I also enjoy the occasional slickly produced and packaged nuggets of rhythmic/melodic processed sugar as much as the next gal, let's never confuse or conflate the work of algorithmically-approved, factory-produced, planned-obsolescent musician-Barbie-widgets with the specter of a joyous, dirty, smelly, complex, confusingly authentic living organism carrying on from a place of instinct, in the rain and sun and ice and snow, come what may. Once in a while it's good to cut out the middleman. Music belongs to everybody: folk, punk, rap, name it. You can get it all bottled up in smooth single-use plastic, but better to find your way directly to the source. Ask around until you locate a spring, and haul your own bucket.

(Lit Hub, 2022)

MAKE IT MEAN SOMETHING

I SPEND a lot of time on Instagram. I'm not particularly proud of this, but I'm also not inclined to disparage myself too harshly for it. Whatever gets you through the night (and/or morning, afternoon, evening). I spend a lot of time on my "phone" in general. How about we start calling it what it is: Hand-Held Computer. HHC, for short.

I do the usual: text, read the news, gawk at people I find genuinely inspiring and admirable, gawk at people I find vaguely or severely dumb, obnoxious, triggering. Gawk long enough at anyone in the first category and they morph into the second. I make lists, deal with email, read recipes, buy train tickets. It's nice to be "productive" in this way whilst, say, lying down. Or walking the dog, waiting in line, stuck on a boring phone call, half-assing yoga. My predilections are not unique. I use my HHC to avoid being alone with my dreadful thoughts. I use it to escape anxiety and uncertainty, to create and embroider community. I multitask like a motherfucker. I use it on the toilet. I use it when those around me are using theirs. I use it while waiting for food to be brought to me. I use it while eating alone. I use it to listen to music and audiobooks. I consult weather, and time, and maps. One screen at a time isn't even enough for me anymore. Often, I'm watching a movie or something *while* dicking around on Instagram. If the movie is particularly good (or bad) I might try to find an artful way of instagramming it. None of this, in the harsh light of confessional essai, sounds great. Apologies to Jaron Lanier and Catharine Taylor and Jenny Odell and whatever other postmodern philosophers are currently urging us not to lose ourselves entirely to the supremacy of our HHCs. I had the cheerful and completely earnest thought, recently, at bedtime, about how when I woke up in the morning there would be a whole new Wordle to do. Ain't life grand?

I am forty-four years old, and eighteen years into a love relationship. We have reared our offspring into young adulthood. Our job as parents now is to step back and hold space. This turns out to be much, much more difficult than I anticipated, especially given the fact that our young adult now lives a great deal of *his* life inside *his* HHC, which he acquired as a gift (from us) for his Bar Mitzvah. Today you are a man: here's your HHC. We held out as long as we could. He claimed he was last among his friends. Godspeed and good luck, young man.

Is it okay to just leave him alone with all his screens all the time, as he seems to somewhat prefer!? Apparently so, assuming he's otherwise happy, healthy, and active, according to some excellent Instagram accounts about parenting teens.

Often, after dinner, each member of our family retreats to a different room to do different things on different screens. Blame the architecture of our 1872 row house, or blame the vagaries of adolescence, or blame the neuroscientists who sold out to the app designers. I don't know. Blame Elon Musk, blame Jeff Bezos. Blame the Netflix honchos. Blame congress for not acting fast enough to regulate social media. Blame the content creators. Blame the influencers. Blame myself. Blame each other.

Can't we just be in the same *room* on different screens, I often find myself whining. And how about a digital sabbath? Could we say that on the seventh day we will refrain from using our handheld computers? One day a week! The other six days we can burn out our eyeballs to our monkey-brained content! Could we try!? The answer, so far, for my family, seems to be... no.

In dealing with my confusion and consternation, I have two options: One, I can spiral into a panic about what's happening to our minds, what's being done to us, and how we're complicit in our own psychic servitude and complacency. I can try to exert some fascist rule over our use of screens; or two, I can accept that life has changed irrevocably—screens are just how we exist now—and leave everyone to it, let everyone off the hook, myself included.

I vacillate. (Oh, but isn't there a middle way? Sure, sure, sure, yeah, yeah, yeah.)

I'm lonely in my little dark corner of the house with my HHC. But I'm also inspired and delighted and engaged and interested and occupied. And bored. And exhausted. And outraged! And invigorated! And amused. Somehow all at once.

Yes, I could quit social media (ideally without announcing it on social media). Yes, I could change my display to grey scale, deprive my dopamine receptors of the delicious colors. Yes, I could go out to a (gasp!) movie theater. But I... don't want to.

In the late nineteen-eighties, when I was a kid, my mother came home unexpectedly one day and found me watching TV. I wasn't supposed to be watching TV on that particular day, or at that particular time. And probably the TV had been an ongoing source of parental anxiety and upset for quite some time.

Long story short, she lost her shit. Accounts vary, and memory is famously unreliable, but I do believe mom picked up a nearby chair and threw it into the television, smashing it spectacularly. I don't have an image of which chair, or what happened afterwards (who cleaned it up?), but I can tell you that we were without a TV for the following several years, which is probably how I got quite so into books, so... Thanks, mom.

The story of the golden calf was given to me (to borrow framing from Clarissa Pinkola Estes) as a story about impatience, faithlessness, and idolatry.

When we tell our liberation story on Pesach, we don't speak of the Israelites as "them," our old-timey ancestors. The Israelites are "us:" *We* are the liberated slaves. *We* were taken out of bondage, and *we* crossed the parted sea, and *we* danced and sang all the way to the other side, where we watched the bad guys get swallowed up, and turned to face the rest of our lives as desert wanderers with a wary eye toward the Promised Land, freedom being just another word for nothing left to lose. "We" followed Moses out of familiar/terrible Egypt and into the vast unknown.

Were we stoic? We were not. Did we forge ahead without complaint? We did not. We were a whiny-ass bunch. We were nostalgic for slavery, for the predictability and "safety" of it. We hadn't eaten *well* as slaves, but we had eaten *reliably.*

And poor Moses. Consider the extraordinary, impossible, toxic burden of leadership. (Keegan and Peele's "Obama Anger Translator" comes to mind.) We need our belief in steadfast leaders like we need air and water. We need our human gods, our idols, our authorities. "Following" alleviates a lot of our anxiety, takes the onus off. We feel better putting ourselves in the hands of someone who seems like they really know what they're doing, where they're going. And it smells good when you're cookin', so whoever everyone *else* is following... has to be worth following, too, right? RIGHT!? Overheard recently in Manhattan: "Ooh, there's a crowd of people in line for something; must be good, let's go see!"

Followers aren't a big riddle. Followers are a dime a dozen. But leaders? The real ones, the decent ones, the ones who don't get high on their own supply? Fascinating, and impossible.

Beleaguered Moses needed a break from all our bellyaching. As any parent of young children who's ever availed herself of, say, a three-day solo getaway will surely understand: Moses needed a breather. You've got to put on your own oxygen mask before you attend to your dependants.' Moses took leave of his irritating, clamorous followers and went up Mount Sinai to "talk to God." A euphemism! Moses watched the Harry and Meghan docuseries on Netflix, ate a gummy or two, ordered room service, and tried a float tank (quite nice). And Moses concluded that Duchess Meghan was right: love absolutely does win.

For forty days and forty nights, Moses is off on his little "creative retreat." He tells his therapist that Mount Sinai is "super restorative." He probably misses his little tribe. He vows to have more patience for them. And he gets some solid work done! Two big, beautiful tablets, engraved by hand with ten basic precepts for living. A relaxed mind is a creative mind. Forty days and forty nights! They say it only takes thirty days to develop entirely new neuropathways and establish new habits.

Meanwhile, what of "us?" The frightened, all-too-human Israelites. Waiting, growing restless, going feral. At loose ends without our leader. Panicked he might not return. Cosmic Daddy figure, God-stand-in, do not forsake us! Yeah, he's probably never coming back. We needed something to hold on to. We needed something to occupy our attention and energy. Something to distract us from the emptiness, the uncertainty, the enormity and exhaustion of our journey. Something to focus on when the unknown was too scary, too overwhelming. A way to pass the time. Something in front of our faces, to look at.

Thus, we built ourselves a placeholder. We melted down our jewelry and such and made ourselves a nice, shiny thing. An idol to dance around in heedless worship. Ahhhh, that's better: Objectification! Much, much better. Tangibility! Everything's going to be okay. What relief! We rejoiced. We partied. We gazed obsessively upon it before sleep and upon waking. We made a thing! Look how shiny. Lookie, look.

And lo, when Moses returned from his sojourn/retreat/quest and saw what we'd done, he got so angry he actually spiked those two excellent tablets, shattering them.

Moses has a little anger problem, don't ya know, a recurrent failure to "regulate his emotions," but this one's not completely on him: apparently HaShem *told* Moses to destroy those tablets. Because we didn't "deserve" them. There's some interesting midrash about *why* Moses was so upset to see us partying with our idol, "God" having already warned him, and all. But to see it with his own eyes must have been "triggering." Zombie Israelites, we of little faith, zoned out on our golden idol.

Relax, Moe. Take it easy, HaShem. It's, like, decoration. It's, like, *art*. It's *content*, bros. Chill.

You don't like how we attempt to entertain and enjoy ourselves and each other while we wait to find out how our individual and collective stories unfold? You don't like how we pass our stupid fucking time? Distraction changes shape and scale. It evolves. We're all on some weird trip together. But okay: You like rules? You want restrictions? You want limits and boundaries? Okay. Alright. Rules can be very useful. Let's make us some rules! But remember: Rules were made to be broken.

I have no real argument for why I prefer Instagram (an amusing bore) to Facebook (an idiotic bore) or Twitter (a sinister bore). Maybe I'm just too impossibly earnestly discerning when it comes to ideas and text, whereas images, colors, jokes, travelogues, memes, outfits, meals, products, and local events are easier to enjoy. More elemental. Less draining, somehow. FB and the Shwit don't suit me. I'm not masochist enough or sadist enough or bored enough or desperate enough or hateful or self-aggrandizing enough for those. Let alone any one of the hundred others that have come to exist since I ceased giving a shit. Forget Tik Tok, which *might* be a concerted effort by the Chinese government to make us... dumber? To each their own. I like images, art, photography, memes, self-deprecation, targeted ads for shit I might want or "need." Shopping! Sales and craft markets and local businesses and action items and social justice organizing and whatever. Instagram! Tell me who I am, Show me what I want. *Tell* me what to want. Give me new ideas about *what* to want. Inspire me to continue on my path. What *is* my path? I'm so lost. Tell me the meaning of life. What's it all for? Oh, cute baby. I'm so freaking lost. Also bored. And lonely. What does it all mean? Looking at other people. Thinking about how I want to be looked at. Hideous and... human.

I do curate ruthlessly, needless to say. Mute! Block! Unfollow! Mute, mute, mute. Nothing can make me endure a garbage feed, one that's nakedly only about ego sans substance or self-awareness, a feed that is only about money or privilege or access. Nothing can make me entertain a feed that is banal or didactic or comprised of too many selfies. Or a feed that is simply reactionary. Or overly self-serving.

I don't care if you once gave me a kidney; I won't consume your bullshit unless I find it genuinely interesting on some level. I won't look at feed that is a blunt attempt at cult of personality. And nothing can make me endure a feed that is one-note or repetitive. Scrolling is still (somewhat) optional! A lot of the tone-deaf, self-righteous, vapid, uninformed, uninspired crap has to gooooo. All you perfectly decent folk who can't take a decent photograph to save your lives: bye. All you perfectly fine folk who blather on and on about yourselves, openly self-aggrandize, leave nothing to the imagination? Sorry, thank you, next. Are you devoid of wit or grace or the power of suggestion? Do you regurgitate simplistic drivel? Love ya but gotta mute ya. Take this shit too seriously? Later, alligator. No hard feelings. There's not enough time even in these here wastelands of time, even in veritable *deserts* of meandering lost time, even in purgatorial *hours* upon *hours* upon *hours* of time time time time tiiiiiiiime. It has to mean something. But you can't try too hard to *make* it mean anything.

Don't worry, though: there remain hundreds, if not thousands, if not *tens* of thousands, if not *hundreds* of thousands, who may well adore your terrible feed. Live and be well. Pander and prosper. I only know how I feel, and what I want. When it bores or irritates me, it's gone. From my *feed*, silly, not necessarily from my *life*. They aren't the *same* (yet). I'll still bring you soup when you're sick, and I might very well still picnic with you in the park. I will return your calls and texts, I just don't want your content. In the realm of the HHC, I am the almighty God of what I allow to parade before my own eyeballs, which might be the only true power left to me on this blighted rock.

Anyway, the wandering, the complaining, the vicissitudes of faith: What's the takeaway? Grow up listening to midrash and you start to think in terms of takeaway. Which is funny, because there are infinite takeaways, which can also mean there is no such thing as a takeaway. Regardless, let's try some on for size: We are malcontents by nature. We are often ungrateful. We are short-sighted and tend to prefer immediate gratification to long-game struggle and effort. When mired in messy uncertainty (which is... always), we are basically spoiled children incapable of tolerating frustration. We'd usually rather be cozy and oppressed than empowered and free. Change is haaaaaaaard. Something about patience. Something about the subversion of the personal and collective ego. Something about waiting.

Everything is itself *and* a metaphor, or any number of metaphors. And as Jews, to improve upon the way-too-frequently cited Didion line, we tell stories *about* stories in order to live. Yes, this is also called overthinking. Is there an entry for "Jew" in the DSMV yet? Shall we take pills to subdue it? Meditation is much too hard.

A few months ago, I deleted the app. *I want my brain back*, I said to a friend, then lasted one whole day (not even) before I downloaded it again, logged in again, and sheepishly posted something I "had" to post. You know, for my "career."

Is it okay to spend an hour of your day looking at your feed? Is it okay to spend two hours a day looking at your feed? Who am I to say what's okay? But what else are you doing with your time? What do the other 23 or 22 or 21 or 20 or 15 or 10 hours of your day look like? Do you still read books at all? *Can* you still read a book? If you *can't* read a book, how on earth might you begin to *contextualize* what you see on your HHC? If you can't read a book, how can you know how to properly *curate* your HHC?

Just be *careful*, I beg my darling teen. Be careful what you give your eyeballs to.

He grew up watching me lost on *my* fucking HHC.

I'm sorry, sweetie.

I bought a muffin with my coffee recently. In NYC on a brief getaway. Ever the flaneur. Not quite Moses on Mt Sinai for forty days/nights, but same general idea. Blueberry muffin. I needed immediate food because I'd slept late, it was pretty much lunchtime, and if I didn't get caffeine and carbs into my body post-haste, I was most certainly going to die. "Bonking", we call that in our family, a verb, which sounds sexual but in fact means you are about to expire from lack of food and/or drink.

The coveted bench in front of the beloved coffee shop was empty, it being long past peak loitering hours, and I made myself at home, shoved muffin into my face, swilled my iced cortado like it was the titty-juice of the gods. The sugar and caffeine hit my blood stream, and I was saved. I was going to live.

I had with me my HHC, a notebook, pen, and novel: *The Lonely Passion of Judith Hearne* by Brian Moore (perfect, depressing, post-WW2 Ireland, TW: "spinster", n-word, alcoholism). I arranged it all beside me, ready to make the most of the sunshine and blood sugar rush and primo bench spot.

But what did I *actually* do? Delved directly into the HHC, allowed myself to be dominated by it, checked all my apps, then checked them all again. Maybe I answered an email, added something to my calendar. Maybe I pruned a list or two. Maybe I texted everyone back and back. Mostly I scrolled Instagram. There was surely some lust or longing involved, some covetousness. A dash of schadenfreude, no doubt. Some envy, but envy can be handily subsumed by a bit of judgment and hatefulness before swinging back around to good old lust, longing, covetousness. Cheap drugs.

Many minutes vanished forever while I ignored the note-book, the pen, the novel, my immediate surroundings, and the remaining half muffin, which I'd carelessly left on the far end of the bench.

Eventually I came back into my body and noticed where I was in time and space, and glanced up to see the half-muffin being swarmed by small birds. First one, then another, then four, then nine. They were going to town on that half-muffin. It was a jolly frenzy, and it reminded me of something. Something about survival, communication. Something about group-think. Something about simple carbs, cheap drugs. Something about group dynamics. I took a few photos, and thought about posting one. But nothing witty enough came to mind for a caption. I couldn't make it mean anything.

(*Smashing the Tablets*, SUNY Press, 2024)

ON NOT GETTING WHAT I WANTED

WHAT I WANTED WAS A BABY. It was not a logical or defensible want. I already had a baby, a dreamy son I hesitate even to mention for fear of exciting the evil eye. But I wanted another one. Another baby. All the mom-people I knew kept having other babies, more and more babies. Everyone knows you have to have *at least* two, otherwise it's not a real family, and why even bother with the whole endeavor in the first place?

We were lust-crazed morons when we had our first baby, but we'd learned so much, risen to the occasion, grown up, evolved, and now we wanted another baby, a celebration baby, to come out of our hard-won stability and contentment.

By "we" wanted, I mean "I" wanted. He wanted another baby, too; claimed he was very much looking forward to the existence of the other baby. But the thing is, he never wept inconsolably when it didn't happen. The inconsolable weeping was all mine. It's really surprising how many tears a person can weep.

I didn't tell a lot of people about my wanting because A) I did *not* want to be defined by it, and B) It hurt so, so bad. Of those I did tell, a few were kind and circumspect, but most were somewhere on the insensitive-to-fucking-asshole spectrum. So it goes. Did you know that there are people in the world who are ravenously eager to pity others in attempting to make themselves feel superior? They're called sadists, and they're everywhere!

It crushed me when people said crappy things, and boy did people say crappy things. Well I'm just so glad *mine* have each other and Don't you think it's cruel to just have one and Only children are weirdos and I know how you feel because I only had three boys when what I *really* wanted was a girl. It was pretty astonishing, how much stupid shit people said to me. A reflexologist said I didn't want it bad enough. A nutritionist said I wanted it too much. A foul douche cousin said I would never trust an only child. Once I overheard a kid from down the street in conversation with my son: "What's it like being an only child? Seems like it would be super lonely." I had to clutch the kitchen countertop, close my eyes, and take an extremely deep breath to stop myself from popping in to be like *Hey kid, what's it like having an alcoholic for a mom? Seems like it would be super toxic!*

Here are the kinds of people who have only one child: people disallowed more under fascist government, coldhearted selfish career-obsessed bitches, people who loathed the experience of having the one, people with biological incapacity, and mothers of such advanced age that having even one was a dystopian miracle.

You have to have *at least* two: Why did I constantly look at other families with multiple children—even when said families were wildly dysfunctional and/or broken and/or blatantly miserable—and think: well, at least they're a *real* family. Need-less to say, I had to mute everyone I know who uses social media exclusively as a means of showcasing offspring. No big loss there, though, and honestly, you guys: cut that obnoxious shortsighted exploitative shit *out*.

Let us pause to remind ourselves, in spite of our sitcom brainwashing and general cultural programming and absurd devotion to some bygone bullshit Rockwellian lie, that *there is no such thing as a formula for a happy family*. Some of every stripe in every configuration manage to fuck it up, and some of every stripe in every configuration manage to rock it. Maybe family happiness exists on a spectrum, like gender. Suck it, Tolstoy.

Anyway, anyway: I wanted a(nother) baby. And when the (other) baby declined to appear, I felt cursed and punished and blighted and tragic and enraged and impotent. I screamed into the void. I told God to eat shit and die. And I found out some interesting things about myself. Such as: I am in conversation with God.

Also: I did not want that other baby bad enough to sign my ass up for fertility treatment. I can almost, but not quite, imagine wanting it that bad. I one hundred percent did not want it that bad. That certainty was like a towering stone wall in my heart. I often rested my forehead against that wall. Its coolness and solidity provided great comfort and reassurance. That wall had always existed, long, long before I did. It was a primordial wall. It was covered in moss. It was an ancient, quiet, verdant, merciful, restful place. I spent a whole lot of time there.

Like I said, I already *had* a baby. A beyond wonderful baby. And still, still, I wanted *another*. How greedy is that? To "want" life itself? The more I thought about it, and hahahaha, man, did I think a lot about it, the more indefensible it seemed.

My job, then, was to learn to surrender want. I threw myself at this monumental task. I wanted to be worthy of it. A badass undertaking. When you surrender want, you join the ranks of priestesses and seers. When you surrender want, you became a guru and a beacon. (But, like, ego-less.) I wanted to be *totally fucking at peace with exactly what is*. I wanted *not* to despise God whenever some odious jerkoff announced the birth of their second / third / fourth / fifth child. I wanted not to care when sadists parroted nonsense to me about "only" children. I wanted not to feel mortally wounded whenever some intimate stranger went on some dumb caption bender about how it's Harlowe's fifth birthday today and goodness gracious we don't *deserve* her but *God sent* her to us and we're just so grateful that she *chose* to *complete* our family or whatever thoughtless nonsense noise.

I wanted not to want. I wanted it so, so bad.

I thought maybe the mikvah (Jewish ritual bath, look it up, I'm not your ethnic shortcut) might help me in my progress toward relinquishment of want. Or maybe... the mikvah would be the magical key to open the door to the desired pregnancy! UGH, so annoying, that reflexive, automatic want! Fuck *off!* I wanted to stamp it out, extinguish it. It caused me nothing but pain. Enough! No more! I was a prisoner of want, and I wanted to be free. Do you see my quandary? Wanting was everywhere.

I have a friend who bore 13 children. I can't even fathom loving 13 people that much. How full can a heart *get?* Most everyone I know recoils in horror at the thought of 13 children, but I stand in awe. Not just because she *bore* 13 children (although, uh, superhero much?) but because she *raised* them all, with strength and decency and humility and love and self-sacrifice, which is something like governing a small country and something like running a school and something like being a top-notch nurse / administrator / teacher / CEO / cook / housekeeper. This woman has her shit *together.*

My friend with the 13 children agreed to tutor me with regard to the mikvah. She gave me books: *Taharat HaMishpacha, Waters of Eden.* I already knew the gist; I'd immersed once before, in advance of a reckless starter marriage at 23, but the real-real turned out to be a fair bit more complex and interesting than I'd previously understood. I read up, and went over to her house on Tuesday evenings to study some more. We sat side by side at her table and read aloud together. She was a good teacher, a gentle woman. There was nothing in it for her.

The laws of family purity get a bum rap for seeming to imply that menstruation is dirty, and that women need to be cleansed/purified because we ourselves are metaphysically dirty/bad. Cue the automatic assumption that religion is inherently misogynistic and all observant women must be an oppressed bunch of self-hating victim/slaves. I believe this to be a pile-up of etymological misunderstanding, but what can I tell you: look at the texts and the texts about the texts and make up your own mind, or don't. No skin off my nose, as the old saying goes. (I mean, a personal no thanks to the part about sending one's used panties to a Rabbi for inspection if unsure about the precise color/nature of vaginal discharge, but to each their own.)

My studies left me dazzled and delighted. To my mind, mikvah is as radically feminist a ritual as they come, and by "radically feminist" I mean: enormously insightful with regard to personal freedom, the rhythm and care and life span of a soul inside a body with an unmediated menstrual cycle, hard truths about fertility, life, and death, and power dynamics within long-term monogamous intimacy.

Sex with the same person for years and years and years gets boring, no matter how much you may adore and respect and like that person. Without mystery and newness and romantic intrigue and the psychedelic dance of courtship, how can you possibly stay jazzed? *Taharat HaMishpacha* has some answers: You quite literally do not touch your spouse for two weeks out of every menstrual cycle. You separate, and then you reunite. Said reunions are glorious. You cherish your weeks "on" and you savor your weeks "off." You take clearly demarcated, finite breaks from being sexually desired and/or desirous. A human being cannot have or be had on every whim.

The mikvah is often described as the marking of transition. A movement from one place—one identity, one role, one state of being—to another. Marital sex, which for me had become routine, an exercise in futility, a hotbed of grief and anxiety and failure, could be thusly honored and reframed. *Yes*, mikvah said: Sex *can* be boring and rote and pointless, and yes, it *would* be easy and fun to find someone new to do it with, but instead *you* are going to become new, which in turn will make your spouse feel new, which will ideally allow you to anticipate and enjoy relations for a long time to come.

Bleeding, which had become the embodiment of heartbreak and injustice, could likewise be thusly honored and reframed. *Yes*, mikvah said: Bleeding *can* be a recurring funereal curse. Now come and enact this ritual that belongs to you and belonged to your ancestors (oh-ho, you thought we were going to get out of here without acknowledging the *ancestors*?), and allow it to wash away heartbreak and injustice, so that you may emerge fresh and intact and whole and fine, just as you are. You are *not* cursed or broken or blighted; you are alive in your very own body, which is, itself, an Eden, holy and sacred and worthy and fine, just as it is.

So, for the first time in years, I visited the mikvah. A little unmarked building in the far corner of the parking lot at my local JCC. How many times had I seen it without registering it, without even wondering what it was. A lovely shomeret was there to observe and assist. I said the brachot and completely immersed, three times, in the collected rainwater.

I won't bore you with tales of mystical rebirth; it's feckin' private. Suffice it to say, everything about it felt good and right. Every bell was rung.

The wanting didn't magically go away, but it did fade some. Wanting's a tricky bitch; it waxes and wanes. Wanting is like an odor; it can find its way through the tiniest cracks. Wanting is like a weed; it self-sows. I am a person of some privilege who came of age in late-stage capitalism, so I am not well conditioned to, like, chillax with not getting what I want. (Dial up cinematic Veruca Salt from the original *Charlie and the Chocolate Factory*: "I want a party with roomfuls of laughter, ten thousand *tons* of ice cream... and if I don't get the things I am after, I'm... going... to... SCREAM!")

I kept thinking I'd return to the mikvah, dip on the regular, make a proper habit/practice of it. But you know how it is... there's soccer practice or the dog hasn't been walked or you're going on a trip or there's an event you have to attend or—whoops—pandemic time. Or you're just beat from trying to meet a deadline or advance yourself in some way or keep abreast with everyone and their mother on whatever platform holds you in thrall.

Still, my awareness continued to shift. I keep distance from my spouse during *niddah*, the days during and immediately after menstruation, and I notice that I tend to instinctively dress differently during that time, too. Less likely to put the precise contours of my body on public display. Less likely to advertise what nice tits and ass I have. During that time, I do not exist for the pleasure or approval or appraisal of anyone else. It's my time to be an independent creative entity, a fundamentally human animal more than a socially constructed and perceived "female" object. (I'm happy to show off my tits and ass the rest of the time, though, rest assured! I'm not like an *anarchist* or anything.)

I'll probably always have a very tender spot where resides the lack of what I wanted, and that's okay. I might even go so far as to say it's *good*. Does the world really need more checked boxes, more acquisition, more staged holiday photos, more general smugness? Have we not seen the devastation wrought by certain classes of people in certain sorts of societies *getting everything they want?*

Not getting what we want can leave us soft, bruised, gentler, quieter, and maybe a little more watchful and humble than perhaps we'd otherwise manage to be. Maybe not getting what we want can make us more grateful for what we *do* have. Isn't that just so nice and tidy? Well, no: it's also hard, messy, awful, and frustrating. It really is quite insanely hard. I still admittedly have a lot of trouble with certain Instagram narratives.

I sigh the lack of many a thing I sought, quoth a Shakespeare sonnet I scrawled on the inside cover of my diary as a lovelorn teen. Back then I was pouting over unrequited love, as yet unschooled in deeper realms of thwarted desire.

I. Wanted. Another. Baby. For a long time, it was impossible to even speak the words out loud: I was too desperately vulnerable. You could snap my spine in half like a twig. Even now, I can type it, but I probably still couldn't say the words out loud. How unfair it seemed, how *wrong* it felt that I didn't get that other baby. Only *losers* don't get what they want. And I really did not want to be a loser. But I also did not want to be lost in a vortex of thwarted desire forever, so. You find ways to move the fuck on, and you thank god you aren't one of those programmed shmucks who think there's some prefab equation for a full or happy life.

By the way! The essential nature of want is that it is infinite and can't ever be fulfilled. Visit an AA meeting sometime and see for yourself.

I know people with two children who yearn for three. I know people with three children who yearn for four. I even know someone with four children who years for five. I wonder if my friend, my kind teacher, the mother of 13, ever indulges in wistful imaginings of what number 14 might have looked like, or smelled like, or how it might have felt to touch her lips to that nonexistent baby's sweet, sweet brow.

(*Wanting: Women Writing About Desire*, Catapult, and Tablet Magazine, 2023)

AUTUMN, ALBANY

THE FIRST TIME I get rear-ended is at a stoplight on the corner of Central and North Lake at 4pm. One minute I'm on my way to school pickup, the next minute I'm disoriented and sobbing.

The at-fault is a nineteen-year-old dude in a Jeep full of friends. He is nonplussed. He asks, without affect, whether I am okay.

"No!" I scream. "What the *fuck?*"

My car is badly damaged and I can't stop sobbing. No airbags deployed. I am worried the dude will get back into his car and flee, so I photograph his license plate in haste, and call the cops. I cannot for the life of me stop crying. My rage and fear and shock are a tangle. The Jeep doesn't have a scratch on it. It's raining. The dude and his friends huddle under a shop awning, laughing.

The cop tells me to calm down: "It's not that big a deal, ma'am." Later, when I call the cop oversight office to suggest that this particular cop go fuck himself, the oversight officer will watch the body cam footage and promise to speak to the cop in question about sensitivity in traumatic situations.

For some reason, I refuse an ambulance. ("Some reason," ha: I am more terrified of institutional health care than I am of getting back into my smashed-up Subaru and driving away with whiplash and a concussion.)

I spend days in bed, in the dark, alternating heat and ice. A haze of phone calls from insurance agents, a hailstorm of Advil, buckets of CBD hot freeze.

You can get rear-ended anywhere. This wasn't Albany's fault, per se. But it's so easy to blame Albany. Fucking Albany! This was God's way of telling me I've done my time in this hopeless shithole of a city, right? Or maybe this was God's way of punishing me for never utilizing public buses. Or maybe this was God's way of shaming me for having my kid in private school. The thinks you think when you're stuck in bed, in the dark, without distraction, for days on end! Meditation is a billion times harder than CrossFit, and "God" is a tough epigenetic habit to break.

A golden, shimmering autumn. Something about the particular precious autumn light. The garden is still mostly green, but a hint of crunch has begun to sneak into the leaves: the beginning of the end. I continue to water the strawberry plant even though there will be no more strawberries this year. If spring is birth and summer is youth, fall is the full bloom of middle age (and winter is death). I'm forty-one, the harvesttime of life. The bright, sunny September of life. Assuming the good fortune of a long life, that is. A stupid assumption.

A trio of young people–in, let's say, the late-June of their lives—moves into the apartment building next door. They're showing friends around their new digs one afternoon, out on the back deck. They high five and shout *PARTY CENTRAL, BABY!!*

"Hey there," I wave from my garden, and they beat a hasty retreat.

I've been living here for a decade. Forty seasons.

Seems like only yesterday I marched into the little house on Jay Street, set down my literal and metaphorical baggage, and decided that, by sheer force of will, this was going to be an *awesome* place to live. Things were going to start *happening* around here. Some iteration of the old Zionist narrative, all that stuff about making the desert bloom. Did I really think that I could, by sheer force of will, by patronizing every open storefront on Lark Street, by walking to the coffee shop every day and making cheerful small talk with neighbors, by *becoming* a regular even though back then I didn't much care for coffee, by inviting people over all the time, by flinging my literal and metaphorical doors wide open—transform what is essentially a raped and murdered corpse of a city, a deeply flawed, systemically undermined/ignored infrastructure-impoverished nightmare of a city, surrounded by complicit, anodyne, deaf-dumb-blind suburbs and exurbs, into some kind of *Eden*!?

You're supposed to move *out* of this neighborhood when you have kids, that's the conventional wisdom. Those of us who won't, or can't, or don't, we cluster in Facebook groups and assure ourselves about imminent improvement, the rising tide that lifts all boats. This is a *wonderful* place to live, we reassure ourselves and each other, the *best* place to live.

But neighborhood booster-ism seems increasingly beside the point when a simple walk around the block is like something out of Mad Max. What does it matter that there's a delightfully twee craft market in the lake house next weekend if to *get* to the lake house you have to hazard a faded crosswalk on a road frequented by an endless succession of irate entitled psychopaths behind an endless succession of wheels, eager to get the hell back to the suburbs or exurbs or wherever. In other words, still no progress whatsoever manifesting better pedestrian safety infrastructure. City Council did finally approve a small budget for putting in some reflectors and a few more signs around the park, but the projected date for installation has come and gone a few times now, and every time I call the police station to request speed patrol, I get the brush-off.

Prioritizing human-scale existence, aka *walking*: Is it a lot to ask? Is it unreasonable!? I'm a broken record about this. Are we really supposed to lock ourselves behind gates and lawns to try and ensure that we don't get murdered by cars!? Is *that* the answer? If you never have to walk anywhere, it *is* a lot harder to get run down by a car. Ride around *in* cars all day every day, yeah, *that's* better. *You* do the mowing down of pedestrians, and you win, right? Because the world is pretty much just a video game at this point?

Asshole Patrol, we call it: trying to get across the barely

marked pedestrian crosswalk into and out of our public park in broad daylight twice a day. I've (mostly) stopped screaming obscenities, but I do still mutter "fucking asshole" under my breath when necessary.

Ommmmm.

And I spend an embarrassing amount of time contemplating how things unfolded in this country/state/city over the past hundred years to enable the dynamic in question. Fuck the cult of the personal automobile. Though it probably wasn't a picnic when the whole town was knee-deep in horseshit, either.

At the park in the mornings and evenings, we're like religious supplicants gathered to pay our respects to the changing light. A childlike adult person walks alone through the park every morning around nine and stops at the flagpole to salute and recite the pledge of allegiance. A young man asks his small brown shepherd *do you have to go potty do you have to go potty do you have to go potty* on a loop, the entire time they are in the field.

Sunrise, sunset. Make meaning, make meaning, make meaning! Why do autumn days feel so uniquely special, sacred, fleeting? The lingering dusks, the sunshine cutting through the cooling air, the cool air cutting through the sunshine. Such pathos in these days! In "my" tradition they're known as the Days of Awe. What do we *do* with these days? How can we make them *last*? They'll be gone too soon, too soon, before we know it, and we are all very certainly going to die. (I hope that's not news.) This is *it*: savor these days like they are all you'll ever get. Because we all know what's coming, don't we?

Winter is coming.

But oh god, no, let's not think about it just yet, no, don't make us contemplate that yet, please. Surely there's more time? Surely we can put off thinking about *that*? We all know it's coming. But can't we just forget about it for a little while longer? Just enjoy these beautiful, golden days? It's just that the beautiful golden days seem to fly by so fast. Sometimes the chill in the air feels merciless.

A well-heeled lady in an administrative office asks me for

my address, and when I give it to her she is startled: "You live right downtown? Right in the city?"

This lady has spent her entire life in the skin-crawlingly wealthy suburb nine miles to the north of our murdered corpse of a city, and it is her conviction that my neighborhood is a blot on the earth, a place to be avoided and ignored by any means necessary, a place where [say it with me in a haunted whisper] *impoverished people of color* live. But lo! I do not *seem* to be an impoverished person of color! I am in lovely knitwear and nontoxic lip-gloss and cool boots!

"Wow," she manages, at length. "Not many people live down there."

Um, a *lot* of people live "down there!?" They just don't tend to be cloistered *assholes*!? (I mean, okay: maybe assholes, but definitely not cloistered.)

What the woman is saying, of course, is that not many people who have the *choice* to live elsewhere live "there." Here. What she is saying is that, given the *choice*, anyone in their right mind would get the fuck out of "there" / here. I shouldn't take this lady's worldview personally. But I take everything personally. Which is too bad for me, though useful creatively. Give me another forty seasons, maybe I'll figure out another way.

Oh, but set aside your cares, forget your woes! It's time for the annual street festival known as LarkFest, which invariably deteriorates from a swell, cheerful, family-friendly block party at 10am to a loud clusterfuck around 1pm, giving way to a batshit bacchanal by 4pm. Then streets lined with vomit and food scraps and trash for days and good luck trying to keep the dog from trying to eat it all.

"This is a really great place to live if you're an alcoholic," someone mutters to her companion on the patio at Café Hollywood.

"Isn't everywhere, though," the companion responds.

A t-shirt: *Albany: A drinking town with a political problem.*

There are not enough "amenities" in Albany, as a real-estate developer once developer-splained to me over farm-to-table cocktails in the Berkshires.

It does get admittedly harder to feign excitement about yet

another new small business with unreliable hours. The poke bar serves decent food but exclusively in single-use plastic. The new bakery barely has any fresh anything and is furnished with folding chairs; it will be vacant in less than a year. The cute little sweet shoppe lasted about six months and then relocated to a strip mall in Clifton motherfucking Park. The Mediterranean bar and grill had themselves a nice sign above the door, a real actual custom permanent sign above the door, wow, look at that, but the place folded almost immediately. Everything feels so provisional. Set up to be temporary, and barely scraping by. With the exception of the artisanal cider donuts on North Pearl, which proved so wildly successful that they just announced the opening of a new location up in mall-death hell, with *plenty of parking*, the press release repeats a couple times. Wouldn't want anyone to break a sweat en route to or from a donut fix. The guy who bought the huge abandoned cold storage warehouse taking up half the skyline made some noise about arts district something-something, but he owes half a million dollars in back taxes and has done nothing to get the building up to code. There's an unfortunately-placed billboard advertising our aforementioned private Montessori school standing proudly up against this eyesore on the highway: poetry in the wild.

But there I go again, focusing on the negative. All those marginally literate new-age feeds I skim must not be sinking in. Hope is where it's at! Hope! Keep it up, against all odds! There's tons of great stuff in this town. The best thrift shop in the world and Elissa Halloran's magical house of treasures and the best coffee shop for a hundred miles and the epic skate shop and the family who makes organic soap and the vegan deli and the woodworker whose custom tabletops feature mosaic representations of housing projects and the cute young couple who renovated and reopened the wine bar and okay yoga and good street art and vintage '90s streetwear shops and local pride, local pride above all, so yes, let's hear it for the 518.

Word travels fast about two armed robberies back-to-back on a Tuesday night around ten. One on our corner, and one on the corner of Lark and Lancaster. We'd noticed a lot of flashing lights and peered out the bedroom window to see what the hell was going on. A few cops walking up and down the block. Nothing too exciting. We shrugged and went back to watching Sacha Baron Cohen play a Mossad spy in Syria circa 1962. A third armed robbery takes place the following Thursday, but this time the cops are on high alert. They immediately catch the perps, who turn out to be children. An eighteen-year-old, two fifteen-year-olds, and a twelve-year-old. The firearm turns out to have been a BB gun. No less terrifying for the victims, but.

The dog has a bad habit of interrogating men who stroll through the field unaccompanied by dogs of their own. The dog finds it necessary to thoroughly question and intimidate said men. THIS IS MY FUCKING PARK, she barks at them. Is it possible that she is the outward manifestation of my private aggression? The dog is an unapologetic misandrist. Some men are unbothered by her interrogation and walk on. The dog respects this. Other men are badly startled, and these men invariably become enraged, which further enrages the dog. It doesn't matter how much I reassure them that she will not bite, that she has no history of violence, that she will not hurt them.

One day, a man with a long grey ponytail in a Siena College baseball cap pulls a knife on me and my barking dog. I stay strangely calm. "She's not going to hurt you," I say. "She is just barking, just ignore her, keep walking, she's not going to hurt you, sir, I'm sorry, but sir, please put the knife away, she is not going to hurt you, I would be glad to leash her up but sir, you are holding a knife out at me, so I'm not going to come any closer until you put the knife away."

He rants and raves and jabs his knife at the dog, who becomes more and more upset. Finally, at wit's end, I take out my phone and inform him that I am filming him now. At this, he walks away, still muttering to himself and waving his knife around. I have zero emotional response until about an hour later, then I'm shaking all day.

On Yom Kippur we endeavor to ride the rail trail, which stretches from Watervliet all the way to Voorheesville. The problem is: how to get to the trailhead, which is three miles from our door. Biking to the trailhead would be the logical way. But those three miles are just about the least bike-friendly you can imagine, so to be remotely safe we'd have to ride mostly on sidewalks, which are all busted up in general. There's the option of driving down to the parking lot at the trailhead. But this makes me petulant, and I refuse on principle. What is the *point* of a local freaking *bike* trail to which you cannot ride your freaking *bike*!? What kind of dystopian nonsense *is* that? We hazard the sidewalk ride.

It's fine-ish until we make it down to South Pearl, the heart of the much-maligned South End, where residents seem possibly outnumbered by vacant homes and storefronts. On one block here last year, a fire started in an abandoned house and destroyed five adjacent homes. There's a convenience store, a streetwear shop, and a wellness studio with, alas, a mold problem. The DMV and a soon-to-close McDonalds cower beneath the grotesque malignancy of 787, alongside which run the good old bomb trains. Whose fault is all of this? Impossible to say, though I'm confident they don't (or didn't) live anywhere near here.

We cruise along on sidewalks, apologizing to the few pedestrians we encounter. Past the police station, Baptist church, Family Dollar, Uncle Dan's Diner, and liquor store, until the sidewalks peter out amidst auto-repair shops, and there's the 787 onramp.

We stop and look around. We consult maps. The trailhead should be right here somewhere, but all we can see is ruins and highway and highway and ruins. To find the trailhead do we really have to cross this half-road-half-onramp with no crosswalk, no light, no pedestrian or bike infrastructure whatsoever?

Indeed, we do. We survive the crossing and what do you know? Immediately past the parking lot it's serene and pastoral. Two minutes later we are coasting south on the trail, wowed by the serenity and peace and abundant beauty of a perfect fall day under canopies of yellow/orange/red trees and the rush of the Normans Kill. Another world. South Pearl is a distant memory from a different dimension.

The moral of the story is that to have this nice experience without having to directly confront the post-industrial late-capitalist nightmare of a failed American city, you should hitch your bike to your automobile and drive directly from your safe exurban or suburban dwelling directly to the parking lot at the trailhead, your feet never having to touch unhallowed ground.

How can I see this place in all its depressing glory and still keep trying to embroider a meaningful life here? I hate it here, and it's my home. It sucks, and it's my home. It has so much potential! But progress and improvement are slow. I want it to be better. I have to believe it can be better. I *do* believe that it can be better. It's my home. One can only bemoan the shittiness of something one believes could be better.

Still, how does change really happen? And when? And what's the difference between nasty gentrification and a rising tide that lifts all boats? Is it just a question of aesthetics? Values? Money?

A suburban teen acquaintance asks my son where he'll go to high school. My son says Albany High. The suburban teen says *Albany High is totally sketchy.*

"What does 'sketchy' mean," my son asks later.

I stumble through a weak attempt at explaining racism and classism and exceptionalism and white flight and privilege and the criminally shitty urban planning and pathetically short-sighted real-estate development and political misdeeds that have shaped this murdered corpse of a city, which is itself so typical of so many cities across our huge, murdered corpse of a country, and in closing reassure him that Albany High is awesome.

Is Albany High awesome? Anecdotal reports are varied, but it had better be awesome, because the attitude of that suburban teen is what's actually sketchy as fuck.

An officer sits in his cruiser today, facing the horrible crosswalk where we try daily not to die. He watches me attempt to exercise pedestrian right of way. The car coming at me from the left slows to a crawl, but the car coming at me from the right makes it clear that it will absolutely not slow.

A reasonable person, hoping to not get hit by a car, might

stop and wait in the middle of the crosswalk for the offending asshole to pass. Might makes right, after all; a body is no match for speeding tons of metal. But I stand firmly in the path of that fucknut, holding up my hand for said fucknut to slow the fuck down and stop. The fucknut does not run me down, thankfully, but he does lower his window and scream, "Get the *fuck* out my way, bitch."

The officer is maybe ten feet away, observing all of this from his cruiser, cup of coffee in hand. As I pass his open window, he tells me, cheerfully: "You really want to wait for drivers to pass before you cross, ma'am."

"That's a pedestrian right of way crosswalk, officer. In our public park. In the heart of our city."

He shrugs. "They really won't always stop, ma'am, and I'd hate to see you get hurt."

"Sir, you're on duty, yes? And you're right here *next* to this pedestrian crosswalk, which drivers are flagrantly disregarding. Do you think it might be *possible* for you to flag and ticket drivers who blatantly disregard traffic laws and endanger lives? Or maybe get out of the car and escort pedestrians back and forth? Your job is to enforce laws, is that right?"

"Just be more careful in the future, ma'am."

Deep thoughts whilst walking the dog around the lagoon (we really need to stop calling it a "lake"): 1. Twitter is a great way to reach people who are always on Twitter. 2. Facebook is a great way to reach people who are always on Facebook. 3. Instagram is just for fun. 4. Time is a bitch, because the sadder you are, the slower it goes and the happier you are, the faster it goes.

I know a lady who moves every few years because no place turns out to be as cool as she'd hoped it might be: Providence, Joshua Tree, Oregon, L.A., Brooklyn, Woodstock, each turns out to be lame, lame, lame. Oh, honey, the places might not be the problem.

The question is not whether or not you *like* living in Albany; the question is whether or not you can do your *work* here. Work is hard and consuming no matter where you do it.

Something about status and money. Something about fashion, ambition. Something about—

Halloween is warm. Throngs of people, big and small. Laughter fills the streets. Dove between State and Lancaster is the best stretch, but Lancaster between Swan and Lark is no joke, either. Everyone is out on their stoops. There is a true spirit of joy and camaraderie. I trail half a block behind my tween and his friend. Everyone's in a good mood. I love this neighborhood. This fucked-up little city *is* the world's best-kept secret. I should be more of a booster. The world is a fundamentally kind and decent place, headlines notwithstanding, and we cannot live separate from our communities.

The youngsters in the apartment next door host a monstrous party that night. A hundred people spilling out onto the back deck. The screaming and laughter and thumping bass keep going past eleven, past twelve, and eventually I call the cops on them.

Boundaries are at issue in a neighborhood like this. Privacy. Anonymity. Which is to say it is a terrible, no good, very bad idea to publish true thoughts and observations and opinions about my neighbors (or my neighborhood). I erased the first version of this essay. Don't shit where you eat. But true thoughts and observations and opinions are pretty much all I have to offer in exchange for money! And I still have to live here. And you have to get along with your neighbors; it's one of the main tenets of human life. Where does tribalism come from? Where does racism originate? What was the earliest iteration of war!? How did moronic bullshit like nationalism ever take root in human consciousness!? Because of being judgmental and cunty to our neighbors, that's fucking how!

I forget to lock my car one night and a homeless man spends the night in it. I'm assuming it was a man, but I could be wrong. There's plenty I'm wrong about. I find the compartments ransacked. The car reeks of ball sweat and cigarettes and booze. Poor dude found nothing of value, just my registration and a dust cloth and some packing tape and fifty copies of a gorgeous inspirational-quote coloring page my son did when he was eight. I thought I'd give those copies away or put them up on bulletin boards around town or something, but never got around to it. *Look Within*, the coloring page said, times fifty. I guess the homeless guy who spent the night in my car did literally that: he looked within... my car. I hope he was cogent enough to appreciate the humor.

The next night, walking down to Post to get an Impossible Burger (yes, I know they're not good for you), we pass a chic, artsy-looking couple walking the other way. Prospectors, it's clear. Casing the town. "It's not as cool as Hudson," the woman says.

Three people are shot in separate incidents on Second Avenue within the course of a week. The mayor goes around with the Chief of Police, knocking on doors to reassure people, and to listen to suggestions about what they can do to help the neighborhood. God, you have to love the mayor. She bought a wreck of an abandoned house nearby to renovate. Also she's a redhead.

There's one convenience store in particular that seems to be the locus of much of the neighborhood activity: good, bad, ugly. *Close down that store*, people tell the mayor. *That store is the source of all our troubles.* But it is the only store left in that corner of the neighborhood. All the other stores have already closed down, because this is, lest we forget, a murdered corpse of a city.

An acquaintance from a nearby storybook weekender enclave posts a photo of Empire Plaza and a derisive caption about how creepy Albany is, and I find myself incited to quick, decisive anger. No, Storybook Weekender, you may not deign to breeze through our (admittedly creepy, admittedly definitive) city monument and define it as such. You do not get to be derisive about our creepy city. That's our job, those of us who live here, in what is our home, which is, in fact, a deeply complex and old and noir and gorgeous and diverse and beset and hopeful and dysfunctional and hideous little city, filled with tens and tens of thousands of people who do not necessarily *get to choose* where they live. Kindly leave the disparaging remarks about our creepy city to us.

This brings to mind the young writer from the city (*the* city) who once paid me a visit. We were having a party, and the young writer, having kept mostly to themself all night, left seeming less-than-pleased. I thought them somewhat rude, but a few days later *I* sent *them* a thank you note. You don't have to be Miss Manners to know that this person owed *me* the thank you note, but I wanted to "close the circle" or something, so I thanked them for coming and wished them well. They offered no thanks in return; just rambled for a while about how great my life seemed, how great that I got to live in the coolest neighborhood in the coolest town, and in such a great house, with such a great community. Everything was so *great* for me, how *great* for me, so *great* for me, so, so, so *great* for me. Lucky *me.* Life wasn't *half* so great in Brooklyn. Life was *hard* in Brooklyn. It was impossible to make ends meet and the pressure was unending and everyone was in it to win it and no one was "real" and there was no community and it was exhausting. I read and reread this note in complete bafflement. Perspective is everything, and nobody ever really knows shit about the precise reality of anybody else's struggle or reward. I sent a link to a list of abandoned houses for sale via the Albany County Land Bank, 'cause you know what? Life *is* great here. So why aren't you lining up to rebuild some small corner of it? Wouldn't *that* be great? There are worse ways to spend your time and energy than saving/maintaining/protecting a tiny corner of the world in the shadow of Rockefeller's arrogant brutalist concrete and marble hellscape for a tiny fraction of what it costs you to live in the glittering cutthroat ultimate metropolis of dreams. Get out a hammer and nail and learn how to use your hands, to paraphrase the Indigo Girls. *Not just your head; you'll think yourself into jail! A refuge never grows from a chin in a hand in a thoughtful pose! Gotta tend the earth if you want a rose!*

Huge snowstorm on December the first. Still technically autumn, mind you. But now there's two feet of snow on the ground. A rare and stunning quiet envelops the neighborhood. School's canceled. The kids go sledding in the park. We let the dog off leash because the whole town is profoundly silent, and she frolics through the powder, weaving around the dumb holiday lights. She might get tangled up in the wires and electrocute herself. If this fucking piece of shit city kills another of our puppies, I swear to God. But she steers clear of the wires and all is well until later, back at home, when she starts vomiting, and becomes lethargic to a terrifying degree. The internet suggests that she is mortally ill from eating too much snow or possibly ice melt, and that she will either die or be fine. Is she going to die? Please don't let her die. Not again. Not another dog done in by this town, please, really. It takes a couple days, and she ruins every rug, but she's fine.

The second time I get rear-ended is at a stoplight, *again*, at 4pm, *again*, by a twenty-year-old dude, again. It's raining, again. I scream *what the fuck*, again.

This time the dude feels *really bad*. This time my car has only cosmetic damage, but his Volvo is all smashed up. "I'm so sorry, ma'am," says the dude. "My brakes must've locked up."

Bullshit, I do not say, *you were texting*.

"My dad is going to kill me," the dude whimpers. "I'm having such a bad day. I lost my job last week. I guess this is how it is: I just can't catch a break."

Dude really wants my *sympathy* right now!? *I'm* supposed to comfort *him*!? *He* can't catch a break? But sure enough, wouldn't you know, the old caretaking instinct rises up and I hear myself going *hey, hey, it's okay, it could be a lot worse, it was an accident, obviously you didn't hit me on purpose, it could be worse, it could be so much worse, it was an accident, everything's going to be okay, you'll see, hang in there, shit happens.*

Whiplash, concussion, sure, whatever, fine, fine, sure, I know the drill. Ice packs, Advil, darkness, fine, yeah. But this time the physical impact is a footnote to the pure distilled emotional blow. This time the message is loud and clear: down on your fucking knees and stay down, bitch. This time, to borrow the tagline of some *Jaws* sequel or other, it's personal.

Rear-ended for the second time in six months, almost to the day!?

"Maybe you're putting out too much negativity and this is some kind of cosmic retribution," says a friend.

"You do have a lot of hostility about cars," my husband notes.

"Maybe you've done your time in Albany," another friend says.

Everyone's right.

Had dinner with a friend down in Hudson the other night. Hoppin' hipster happenin' Hudson. Such a relief to spend time in hoppin' hipster happenin' Hudson. Why? Because of the fine dining, the sartorial glamour, the aspirational edge, the people watching, the cutting-edge amenities! Because of the way money and poverty do this interesting masquerade, this tense dance, this stylized gliding right up to and around each other in a way they simply don't in many other places. Shit: maybe this whole thing, this whole gripe, this whole meditation, these forty seasons, this whole observational *essai*, might really just have been a cri de couer about class all along. In which case I haven't scratched the surface of the truth.

Anyway, my friend spoke about the intense throngs of hoppin' hipster happenin' visitors who flood Warren Street on the weekends to prospect and shop and eat and drink and see and be seen. The crowds are intense and unpleasant and uncool.

"It's unbearable," she said. "People are starting to talk about moving to Albany."

(Longreads, 2020)

ACKNOWLEDGMENTS

Thank you to the editors who commissioned and helped shape many of these pieces: Sari Botton, Sara Kramer at New York Review Books, Robin Romm, Kelly McMasters, Melville House, Sara Lippman, and the Philip Roth Society.

Thank you Leza Cantoral, Christoph Paul, and Kaitlyn Kessinger at CLASH for your passion, commitment, and attention to detail.

Thanks Sam Axelrod, epic peach, for delightful sensibilities, the Hoagland poem, introducing me to R. Schiff, and calling out my overuse of the word "absolutely."

So very fortunate to be in Sarah Bowlin's stable.

Namaste my beloved friends: cyclical bitching is cathartic and I couldn't get through life without you.

Love and gratitude to my parents, stepparents, in-laws, and sibs, including Allison Rudy and Heidi Factor.

Carebear, you are a wonderful dog.

Eduardo and Miller D, I love you "to the most."

ALSO BY CLASH BOOKS

THE MISEDUCATION OF A 90S BABY
Khaholi Bailey

HOW TO GET ALONG WITHOUT ME
Kate Axelrod

ALL THINGS EDIBLE, RANDOM & ODD: ESSAYS ON GRIEF, LOVE & FOOD
Sheila Squillante

VAGUE PREDICTIONS & PROPHECIES
Daisuke Shen

GENDER/FUCKING: THE PLEASURES AND POLITICS OF LIVING IN A GENDERED BODY
Florence Ashley

PROXIMITY
Sam Heaps

WITCH HUNT & BLACK CLOUD: NEW & COLLECTED WORKS
Juliet Escoria

LIFE OF THE PARTY
Tea Hacic-Vlahovic

THE BULGARIAN TRAINING MANUAL
Ruth Bonapace

WE PUT THE LIT IN LITERARY

CLASHBOOKS.COM

FOLLOW US

IG
X
FB

@clashbooks